BOND

BELONGING *and the* **KEYS TO INCLUSION AND CONNECTION**

GREG MORLEY

Copyright © 2024 Greg Morley, BSL International

Book Design and Interior by Damonza

All rights reserved. This book or any portion thereof may not be reproduced or used in any manner whatsoever without the express written permission of the publisher except for the use of brief quotations in a book review.

Printed in the United States of America

First Printing, 2024

hardcover ISBN 979-8-9894562-0-8

paperback ISBN 979-8-9894562-1-5

eBook 979-8-9894562-2-2

Praise for *Bond*

"In *Bond*, Morley presents the antidote to the strains of dissonance widely experienced in today's world of work—*human connection*. He is trustworthy, timely, and transparent."

—*Dr. Kirk Snyder, Professor and Chair of Business Communication, University of Southern California*

"It takes a village to raise DEI! But Greg is one individual whose mastery of creating and leading the bonds that form the most productive teams can make us all better. *Bond* is a compendium of emotional resonance and actions that both electrify our modern-day humanity and return us to our roots of connection. As he writes, 'connection culture is here'—and it must stay. Well-lived and well-written!"

—*Bev Jennings, Founder & CEO, SEE Company, Inc., and Author of* See and Believe: Inclusion and Vivid Transformation for Individuals and Companies

"We are social creatures at the core, wanting and needing connection with others in so many ways—at work, at home, in life. Through provocative stories and practical tools, Morley delivers an inspiring blueprint for staying connected."

—*M. Najeeb Ahmad and Scott R. Willett, Ph.D., Principals, Pennington, and Co-authors of* Surge: Changing Everything with Your Rare Time and Space

"Greg speaks from the heart and awakens spirit as he shares his hard-won insights. Inspiring as it is informative, *Bond* is a must-read for anyone wanting to crack the code on what it means to create true inclusion. There isn't a better person to teach us how to foster belonging than Greg Morley."

—*Susan MacKenty Brady, CEO, Simmons University Institute for Inclusive Leadership*

"In a world of ever more polarizing voices, in *Bond*, Greg Morley brings us back to the core promise of diversity, equity and inclusion—and why it matters to the bottom line. Employees want to work in companies and with colleagues where they can be seen, valued, heard, and respected. And clients want to work with companies who lead with integrity and share their values. I've seen it in action in our work in Out Leadership, with companies and CEOs around the world—where these behaviors are valued, success follows. *Bond* reminds us that belonging matters to individuals and the bottom line."

—*Todd Sears, Founder & CEO, Out Leadership*

"Early on, so many factors challenge our security and trust in others and our place in this world. When we find passion in our work, we just want to contribute and connect—we want to be our best, which is in part, grounded in belonging. Greg Morley's book, *Bond*, is a captivating billboard we all need to stop and pay attention to. A glance won't do. It can literally change your life today."

—*Halena Cline, Artist, and Co-Author of Eating Paint: An Expressive Life*

"Greg's book resonates deeply with its exploration of the concept of 'bond'—a word packed with immense power. It delves into personal depths and ignites conversations about the importance of belonging in the workplace, a topic I passionately advocate for through heartfelt dialogues with young individuals. Every leader should prioritize adding this book to their reading list. From its first page, *Bond* delivers a compelling punch of intrigue that aligns with our inherent understanding. It's a call to rediscover the essence of bonding. Thank you, Greg!"

—*Brianna Birdwell, Leadership Advocate and Author of* Metamorphosis of Misfortune: A Path to Power

"The other four-letter title I would give Greg's book is HOPE. Hope for connecting and belonging throughout businesses in every corner of the world. Isolation is literally killing us. Leaders: Make it stop. Greg's sensitivity toward different cultures threads the needle to weave a tapestry of high productivity, engagement, and retention modern workplaces desperately need. When bonds are unshakeable, anything is possible."

—*Todd Weiler, Assistant Secretary of Defense under President Barack Obama, and Author of* Radical Equality

"Greg's ability to address a subject that has become a cultural norm with clarity of personal experience is masterful. His insightful stories allow the reader to better understand the progression and evolution of one of the most talked about subjects in our society today! His courage and fortitude are exceptional."

—*Elliott Wislar, CEO, Clearbrook, and Author of* Voyage to Victory: Stories and Strategies for Resilience, Risk and Reward

"What truly matters every single day? People! As a leader, my responsibility is to make all feel valued, recognized, and understood, not simply enforce rules and expectations. Greg's eloquent approach to delivering the keys to connection does not waver from engaging storytelling. The interviews are profound. The rare insights into different work cultures and teams will leave you spellbound."

—*Maureen Lippe, Former Editor of* Vogue *and* Harper's Bazaar, *Author of* Radical Reinvention

"Let's get real about belonging. It is not just a romantic notion. It is as essential as breath to our physical and mental health. Some of us know what it's like to grow up without acceptance; however, in the workplace, it's unacceptable for anyone to experience this. Difference sparks innovation. Bonds guarantee results. Greg has written a book that will endure. His insight on various cultures is timely and enlightening."

—*Mat Bunch, MPA, Renewable Energy Generation Grid Reliability Leader, and Author of* Wanted: From Child Homelessness to a Death-Defying Search for Love and Belonging

Contents

Acknowledgments viii
Introduction: Connection Culture Is Here 1
Chapter 1: An All-Inclusive Journey. 7
Chapter 2: Risk and the Real You. 15
Chapter 3: Seeing, Believing, Bonding 27
Chapter 4: Luxury is in the Diversity 47
Chapter 5: Ceilings Are Made of Bamboo, Too 59
Chapter 6: Discoveries of a Lifelong Learner 69
Chapter 7: Lovely to Hear 87
Chapter 8: We, the Dream Team 99
Chapter 9: Safe and Celebrated 115
References 119
About the Author 126

Acknowledgments

For Halloween at the age of five, my parents dressed me up as Superman. When I look back on those pictures, I see a happy, confident, little guy who was encouraged to take on the world, where there would be no limits to what I could do or where I could go. It is that unconditional and encouraging love and support for which I am forever grateful. Positive and practical, my parents supported and encouraged my sister, Beth, and me to explore the world and all its possibilities.

Throughout the process of writing this book, I have thought often of where I came from and where am I going. When I was younger, I imagined writing travel articles and books about faraway places, interesting people, and exotic cultures. Turns out, I did write that book, without pictures of palm trees, sandy beaches, and dreamy mountains. This book is, indeed, a journey of experience, cultures, and community. Even far away from home, one can feel included and have a sense of belonging. For me, that came from always knowing my family was there for me. I am blessed with a supportive husband, Shawn Hiltz, with whom I have a loving life and home. More than just providing me with support, Shawn complements my life, making me a better colleague, leader, friend, and member of my community.

Since starting this book, much has changed. Shawn and I left Hong Kong, our home of seventeen years, and relocated back to Paris. We lost our lovable dog and companion of thirteen years, Lewis. I left the full-time corporate world after more than three decades and took the leap into a new chapter of personal growth. And to close out the year, my mother passed away peacefully following a nearly ninety-three-year long and epic life. All of these events reinforced the core belief in this book, which I have lived, and I am sharing with you. Connections matter. Inclusion matters. A strong sense of belonging matters. Bonds matter. Change and loss are inevitable in life. Having the warm arms of others to fall into and manage change with you makes life beautiful and there is no substitute for them. Be those warm arms to others—your family, friends, colleagues, and community. Even with all that has occurred and because of the bonds I have in life, I still find myself getting the butterflies of excitement and anticipation in my stomach when I reconnect the bonds of the past and as I build the new ones in the chapters ahead.

My most sincere gratitude goes to Candi Cross, who guided me through this project. I could not have done this without her. I am grateful for those who participated in the book with inspiration and insights, along with gracious early reviewers. These people make me so excited for tomorrow and all the days to follow.

BOND

Introduction
CONNECTION CULTURE IS HERE

"But let there be spaces in your togetherness and let the winds of the heavens dance between you. Love one another but make not a bond of love: let it rather be a moving sea between the shores of your souls."

—*Khalil Gibran, poet*

YOUR BRAIN IS better with connections. Your in-built social component stimulates attention and memory, and it strengthens our lifespans, immune systems, neural networks, and cognitive sharpness. Pleasurable company can transmit two important chemicals—dopamine and oxytocin (the "love hormone"). What is happening in our brain can translate into a surge of joy, confidence, productivity, and goal achievement. This is only the beginning of the benefits of your brain feeling positively engaged and supported by others.

Social or group living is said to have preceded pair living by 35 million years, so bonding is at the core of human experience from the earliest days of humans. Human bonds are not only a desire, they are a demand from your body like food and water. Scientist Matthew Lieberman asserts in his book, *Social*, that social pain is as real as physical pain. "Across many studies of mammals, from the smallest rodents all the way to us humans, the data suggests that we are profoundly shaped by our social environment and that we suffer greatly when our social bonds are threatened or severed," Lieberman told *Scientific American* for Gareth Cook's timely piece, "Why We Are Wired to Connect". "When this happens in childhood it can lead to long-term health and educational problems. We may not like the fact that we are wired such that our well-being depends on our connections with others, but the facts are the facts."

Another fact is that although I am an advocate for a return to fundamental bonding and the formation of more bonds—which we are perfectly designed to need and do as humans—I am not a social scientist nor am I a relationship expert. Having worked for celebrated global brands and pioneered diversity and inclusion and human resources programs for over three decades, my mission is to bolster belonging and to highlight the significant value inclusion and belonging bring to individuals, organizations, and society. I know firsthand that a sense of belonging is critical to our survival and to the advancement of subsequent generations. As a leader touching many countries and many cultures, I've witnessed the shocking burden of not belonging and the astonishing value that belonging has created on many levels. It's the difference between depleted and defeated, to superpowered and superhuman results and relationships.

If inclined to dismiss the workplace as simply the door to individual productivity and financial gain, think again. As of the writing of this book, the surgeon general of the United States, the most senior health professional in the U.S. Government, declared loneliness a lethal pandemic, equating it to smoking fifteen cigarettes a day. Organizational psychologist Constance Hadley, who has been researching workplace relationships since she was a graduate student, found that many people are lacking collegiate support and they are not calling it loneliness…at first. She describes workplace loneliness as "a distressing gap between the level and quality of social interaction that you get while working and what you're hoping for. It's a lack of social fulfillment."

Importantly, "it's the feedback from the environment that creates loneliness," she adds. In other words, the responsibility of painting the landscape for people to feel accepted, included, safe, and valued falls to the leader. Then all managers must tend to the gardens of community. Today, this community consists of hybrid workers riding the modified office work week and employees contributing across many countries.

Work Is Connection, Not Competition

If your job or career is extremely or very important to your overall identity, you bond in this way with four out of ten workers (39%) surveyed by Pew Research Center in March 2023. If you possess a postgraduate degree, that percentage goes up to 53%. A sense of belonging is likely instilled in your devotion, performance, passion, and pride in what you do and how you lead. If you are a solo entrepreneur, the ties you experience could be from the dynamic output with clients, industry organizations, and peers in your field, among others.

The workspace should be a safe space. It should be a place where individuals can be their best, feeling accepted, valued, respected, recognized, and heard. A colleague who was very successful in her role was wanted back at home for what her family called "woman's responsibilities". She was in a great deal of conflict because at work, she could challenge herself in unique and fulfilling ways. She received nurturing and encouragement in a professional setting, and she thrived. To state that she belonged at work and "not" at home may sound harsh and judgmental, but in her case, her professional abilities were protected and lauded, leading to one promotion after another and building her professional narrative. She developed her reputation as a strong, empathetic mentor and sponsor who created groundbreaking programs. The organization bonds over telling the story of her legacy embedded in innovations that serve their people. Stories are an instant way to connect and empathize.

All types of professionals are recognizing and implementing storytelling as a device for both cultivating engaged, productive teams and a culture that cares. Since some of our tightest bonds are with our pets, consider the research on *narrative medicine*. Karen Fine, DVM, is the author of *Narrative Medicine in Veterinary Practice: Improving Client Communication, Patient Care, and Veterinary Well-Being*. She defines narrative medicine as "a medical approach which maintains that a patient should be viewed as an individual rather than an example of a disease process," which can be done using a narrative.

By using this approach, she explains, "We are better able to provide customized, effective care." Sound familiar? Rita Charon, MD, PhD, describes narrative medicine in human medicine as "the ability to acknowledge, absorb, interpret, and act on the stories and plights of others" as part of patient care. We've all visited our busy physicians and quickly assessed if they are treating us based on the familiarity with our personal health narrative or taking a formulaic fifteen-minute approach.

When you propel diversity, equity, and inclusion (DEI) forward in personal narratives, it is easier for people to engage in the tenants of belonging rather than drop the principles, which causes misalignment and isolation. Telling a story tends to coalesce everyone, as the natural next act is to listen for common ground and an emotional spark. Of course, stories can be tragedies and what I consider inhuman versus human.

A recent story underlines the point. Many of us know the harrowing tale of fifty Venezuelan asylum seekers who arrived in the U.S. in September 2022. Florida's governor directed them to be put on a plane with the promise of work and housing opportunities in "sanctuary destinations". A stunt without regard to these individuals as human beings. They weren't armed with anything but hope. They boarded the plane without a toothbrush, money, or clothes, but with the promise something would be at the other end, yet nothing was at the other end. They arrived in Martha's Vineyard without any advance notice or preparation. They were not illegal aliens. They were legally permitted to remain in the U.S. while pursuing asylum. I believe these people wanted to belong to the collective story of the American dream. Except for those who wish to destroy the choices and opportunities that dream constitutes, *who* would not want to be included in that dream?

Inclusion is a positive practice of life and leadership, to be sure. If you think deeper into all the ways the past few years alone have tested us – taking us to the edge of our very survival in many places—you will probably come to the same conclusion that division and isolation will get us nowhere in solving any seemingly insurmountable, profound challenges. We need all brains belonging and thinking. Our connection will power the electrical currents of our greatest potential yet to be realized and displayed. The stories and strategies herein will get us closer to the big reveal.

Aren't you as curious as I am?

Chapter 1
AN ALL-INCLUSIVE JOURNEY

"There is no greater agony than bearing an untold story inside you."

—*Maya Angelou, memoirist*

My concept of belonging had few restrictions on me growing up. As a young child, I had two friends who were twin brothers, Puggie and Peewee, who happened to be Black. I thought more of their names than I did their color. Living on a street with mainly White families, I never had a sense of people being so different that you couldn't be friends. My parents did not talk about neighbors in classifications, they were our neighbors. Diversity was quite normal. In her late twenties, my mother lived in Saudi Arabia and traveled through Asia. She taught our family that difference was exciting, not scary. My parents traveled a lot and encouraged my sister and me to travel early in life, which would naturally assemble various connections and perspectives from those places.

Chapter 1

I have a core group of friends from college at the University of Richmond in Virginia. Even after we graduated, we have remained close. Because I went to integrated schools growing up, it wasn't until university when I truly understood the expression, "those on the other side of the tracks." In Richmond, the Civil War was part of the regular discussion, and not just as a historical fact as was treated where I was raised. It was an eye-opening experience.

One incident in my fraternity shook me out of my happy kaleidoscope. Most close friends my age were Northerners, coming from New Jersey, Massachusetts, and Pennsylvania, and every year, the fraternity in which I was a member conducted an intake of new joiners called *Rush*. It was done in a social circle, and it included a mixture of good and bad interactions. One rushee, Alvin, wanted to join. My friends and I were keen to welcome him because he was fun and smart. We thought he would be a great addition. He was very interested in joining the fraternity and the more we knew him, the more we wanted the same for him. What we were not prepared for was the discussion at the meeting where nominees are put forward. He was rejected. He was rejected because he was Black. My friends and I were shocked and hurt—for him, for us. Race was not a subject most of us had really engaged in before this moment. It saddened me that human beings viewed others through this lens, yet I should have been more aware of it earlier. I was also so hurt that people whom I otherwise liked and respected shared such deeply held beliefs, which prevented them from accepting someone with a different skin color into our "club". Of course, I knew this type of thing existed, I just always believed it was a problem distant from my own life and reality.

Today, one of my friends who was part of the resistance to that member joining our fraternity, admits that his view was unacceptable and regrettable, and he's able to talk about it with me. He explained that this was how he was raised. Until confronted by other perspectives, why wouldn't someone maintain the views they were taught? You must genuinely try in even the most extreme circumstances to stand in other people's shoes. They come from somewhere. They have that view somehow. Just because my professional title says "diversity" as an occupation doesn't mean others are going to change because of me, or that the organizations I work for or associate with are entirely diverse and inclusive, but I must own my part that's governed by my mission of inclusion and impact every day.

I wasn't exposed to diversity and inclusion as a field—a necessity in society; a role and responsibility to be managed—until I was out in the early 1990s. I was twenty-eight years old. Socially, I always felt like I hadn't met the "right girl" even though deep down I knew was attracted to men. There was so much societal pressure, I had to unwind my thinking. Thinking of myself in nontraditional ways. Remember also, it wasn't until the '90s that gay rights began to be on the forefront of political conversations and actions to eliminate discriminatory violence (or "hate crimes") in communities. The majority was slowly waking up to realize that LGBTQ people were entitled to the same rights as anyone else.

Years passed, and I "never found the right girl". I was visiting friends in Richmond, Virginia where I had attended university. A close friend asked, "Have you ever thought that *maybe* you are gay?" Your friends must know you well to know that would be an acceptable line of questioning. I had, of course, considered the fact that I was gay, yet I was conflicted. The most important thing to me was that sense of belonging, to my family, within my group of close friends and to the company where I worked. When posed with that question from my friend, I saw an opening and a path of acceptance and greater belonging. This could have gone a few ways to change my compass of feeling love and belonging. She was letting me know I belonged. I went from that conversation to being totally out to my closest friends a couple days later. That self-awareness, affirmation, clicked.

It took a bit longer with my parents, yet they came to accept me for me and know that they had raised someone whom they would always love and respect. It wasn't a mother's love that convinced me I was safe to be me. She could have still loved me and rejected this part of me, which is all too common. It started that way, yet coming out was an event in the lives of my immediate family members that eventually drew us closer. It allowed us to grow in respect for one other, as our uniqueness made us tighter as a unit. My mother asked me, "Why would you choose such a difficult lifestyle?" Where could I even begin forming an explanation of 'choice'? Gratefully, my sister had spent several years working in Washington D.C. and in a restaurant with predominantly gay clientele. She had a diverse group of friends. She was always accepting of who I was, which helped in many ways.

The banter that ensued with my friends following my coming out was enlightening. A back-and-forth of curiosity about being gay on prime display with the usual questions: "When did you know?" and "Who are you dating?" Uncomfortable at first, yet each inquisitive question reinforced my sense of belonging with my friends even more than before. Let's not forget that bonding starts in the womb. If I walked into my workplace feeling abandoned by my family and friends while leading teams, it could have been a massacre of poor decisions and directions due to my misalignment. You can only compartmentalize for so long. Even if you don't look back at the accident, you still leave a trail of damage. How do you want to be remembered? It's a question I constantly ask myself and not necessarily from the vantage point of death—as in, *in remembrance*—I mean from the vantage point of every day I'm blessed with. What impact do you want to leave on others? What gifts that were given to you will you pass on to others?

I spent seventeen years at The Walt Disney Company, and from the moment I joined the company in the late 1990s, I understood diversity to be something highly supported by the company. I was immediately drawn to it.

A June 2020 piece in *McKinsey Quarterly* says, "…while diversity and inclusion have climbed corporate agendas over the past decade, many LGBTQ+ employees continue to face discrimination, discomfort, and even danger in the workplace. When it comes to true inclusion, everyday interactions with peers and leaders matter as much as organizational policies or formal processes. In short, your company may not be as inclusive as you think it is." I know this to be true, and those everyday interactions start with me. Particularly from a global perspective, I'm aware that many people are still not out in the workplace.

The same piece in *McKinsey Quarterly*, "LGBTQ+ voices: Learning from lived experiences", points to four complexities of coming out at work:

- *Coming out is especially challenging for junior employees.*
- *Women are far less likely than men to be out.*
- *Coming out is more difficult for people outside Europe and North America.*
- *People who are open about being LGBTQ+ often have to come out repeatedly.*

I try to remember these realities in every work setting and remain consistently welcoming to all equally. Everyone is on their own journey.

My all-inclusive journey started with me being exposed to diverse ways of being as little humans. Having friends like Puggie and Peewee ultimately instilled compassion, kindness, open-mindedness, and empathy. They had a different background, which I was taught to respect. Rambunctious and always laughing at each other's antics, which I still remember to this day, sowed the seed for celebrating these differences and even seeking them out at every stage of my life.

The journey of inclusion can start at any time. It doesn't have to be neatly traced to childhood where the building blocks of making others feel that they belong fit nicely together like puzzle pieces. In fact, limited beliefs and biases also start young on the journey—between the ages of three and seven—creating a drag on our evolution. We don't know this as children. We can't discern. But even without that discernment, we were prone to be ourselves as we handily drew from our wild imaginations. We said and did what we were compelled to say and do. We dressed and expressed ourselves in mismatched ways to show our unique personalities (when parents and teachers let us, at least!). Play day was every day.

As adults, professionals, and leaders, risk is a daily reality. Sometimes it is a reckoning before all parts of us come together in powerful reconciliation. Let's explore and discover the ways to bond with ourselves, our light, for the most positively influential outcomes.

Chapter 2
RISK AND THE REAL YOU

> "The way we experience the world around us is a direct reflection of the world within us."
>
> —*Gabrielle Bernstein, motivational speaker*

WHEN YOU ARE fortunate enough to have the right people cross your path at the intersection of a major transition, it can give you the injection of courage you need to make good decisions. After all, there are usually others in your life encouraging you to *GO*. They, too, are affected by your choices and direction.

I met my friend and trusted advisor, Susan Brady, when I was leaving Hasbro and joining Moët Hennessy. Susan, who is the CEO of Simmons University Institute for Inclusive Leadership, has tackled the subject of belonging and authenticity throughout her career and published works. She taught me that the heartbeat of my career needed to be *purpose*. After accepting that for myself, I have passed that along to many.

Chapter 2

Offering twenty authenticity strategies for *Psychology Today*, prolific wellness author Tchiki Davis, Ph.D. writes: "Authenticity and purpose are closely linked: A deep sense of purpose can help you to express your authenticity, while developing authenticity will often help you discover your purpose! You may discover the courage of your convictions and want to burst forward with passion to accomplish some worthy goal that moves you deeply enough to champion some particular sort of positive change."

Your purpose is the ultimate anchor when your internal alarm sends signals that you are risking too much being the real you in terms of what you say or do as a leader. Name it "North Star", "True North", "Calling", "My Point in Life"; when you've identified your central life aim of making a positive mark on the world in your unique way, daily ownership of it—along with execution of subsequent, repeatable steps—builds your confidence and resilience. The very nature of identification is gratifying. At the same time, since that purpose is coming from an internal landscape only you are made of, it's safe to say manifestation requires those individual parts that are uniquely yours. In other words, no one else can fulfill your purpose. Case in point: This book in your hands represents my purpose of spreading the message of belonging and ultimately, helping leaders and teams cement a culture of belonging that outlasts annual reports, leadership or strategy changes, and seasons. *Bond*, as a revealing written record, requires me to share my own raw, lived experience and learnings. I'm exposing personal episodes and psychological vulnerabilities.

What's the risk?

The answer is complicated, but Tchiki Davis's distinguishment of *adaptive self* and *authentic self* sheds some light on the answer and pulls us closer to our truth. She explains, adaptive self is "the self that prioritizes fitting in, getting along, and generally doing what we're told. This self is not without value and purpose—it helps us be functioning members of society. But if you're feeling inauthentic, the adaptive self is running your life."

When I think about instances where I may have employed my adaptive self, it may have been either intentional or unconscious. Still, fragments of the real me were not displayed to the intended audience. I may have dodged judgment, yet I also may have missed out on a genuine response, depth of exchange, or the next level of relationship. If we've been judged in the past, we're following internal protocol of keeping protective barriers in place that may not serve us any longer.

Emotional connectivity and context (i.e., all emotional intelligence) are also subjective. This underscores the importance of meeting individuals where they are. One's authenticity isn't governed by another's. *Just be you* is...just that. The risks:

- *Going against cultural norms of a particular setting or population and not being accepted*
- *Being misperceived or misunderstood to the point of losing out (on an opportunity, partnership, etc.)*
- *Saying too much and offending someone*
- *Saying too little and missing out on resonance that could prompt action*
- *Sounding naggingly, intolerably self-serving; "authentic me" necessitates redundant use of "I" and "me", to start*

Davis adds: "To reclaim your authenticity, you need to discover your 'Authentic Self'—the self that prioritizes living according to your values, pursuing your purpose, and fighting for the causes you care about."

I was having a discussion with a forty-one-year-old woman on my team around why she took the position she was holding and how it fit into her whole life, not just her career. As I said to her over lunch, "Purpose creates simplicity, and it guides how and where you invest your energy."

I could sense that she was refreshed after our conversation. At the same time, it also occurred to me that I had more years of life experience that have allowed me to become stronger in my purpose and to ground me in being comfortable as myself in a variety of work settings. Did she struggle with exhibiting parts of herself that could actually enhance her work performance? Yes, as many people do. Nevertheless, we formed a bond from that exchange. I have enjoyed watching her grow and make tough decisions along the way to manage her career and life to ultimately thrive.

Keys to Inclusion
Tracy Spears on "Shifting Out Loud"

Tracy Spears is the founder of the Exceptional Leaders Lab. She specializes in developing leaders, inspiring teamwork, and enhancing inter-office communications. Much of the innovative content in her keynote speeches and workshops are taken directly from her bestselling books, *What Exceptional Leaders Know* and *The Exceptional Leaders Playbook*. Her energetic and interactive approach has helped leaders and aspiring leaders all over the world improve their leadership skills, their communication, and their understanding of how people and organizations succeed. What intrigued me most about Tracy is her podcast, "Shift Out Loud", designed to inspire anyone to play bigger. And I dare say, she helped me to aspire to make my own shifts louder!

Here, Tracy describes keys to inclusion.

Know the new rules of engagement and the difference between intention and impact.

Sometimes we don't realize when we fail to create a safe place for conversation. I'm surprised on both sides—companies that are nailing it and others that are lagging. Well-intentioned people would at least say, "Oh, what I said landed like that?" The CEO of one company that we've been doing a lot of work with called and said, "We want to drop 'equity' from our core values." After we hung up and discussed their new intentions, we sent them a note saying, "After reflecting on your new direction, it is probably best we part company." We just didn't want to be part of anything that's going to take a step back."

A lot of work I do is creating the impact-intention conversation. There is still a reticence to try to put metrics to diversity, equity, and inclusion. How do we quantify it? How do we measure it? I don't think anyone has mastered it yet, so that's an opportunity. What we don't measure doesn't get changed. We know that. The equity piece of those conversations is still clunky, but I'm encouraged by what I have seen over the last few years. It has gone from being a passion and the "right thing to do" to a project to being a strategy for organizations. We are now even seeing organizations weaving it into their core values.

Inclusive leadership starts with the CEO.

If it lives with the HR person and not the CEO, I get nervous. We experience CEOs who say hello, not bother to even introduce us, then leave the room. I've had that happen before. I did a session with a global company of 60,000 people joining by livestream. The CEO met me in the hallway and said, "Listen, I'm not going to sit in but wanted to say hello." That's a moment of truth. It's happening. The cameras. How do I play this right now? I said, "It would be great from a visibility standpoint if the cameras showed you there." He ended up staying and that impacted the organization more than any speaker talking to his team. In smaller companies, some CEOs believe this is an HR project. Those dynamics have changed dramatically over the last two years. I'm optimistic.

Listen for how you can connect to the other person.

I'm weirdly open to anyone saying anything, trying it on and seeing if I can learn from it. I have a wide filter from the beginning. I will be reading *HBR* and *People* at the same time! CEOs don't want to make mistakes, but it's inevitable and human. It endears people to you provided you circle back and talk about the mistakes. That's a powerful piece to consider in the messages you're crafting.

Encourage real-time feedback loops.

I do a lot of training in Shanghai and Singapore. My first time in Shanghai, I did not encourage real-time feedback and at the end of the day, I was debriefed on all the things they disagreed with culturally. I was exhausted. Eight hours and none of the participants spoke for fear of me being the "authority". There had been no feedback when I asked for it. Now, in adapting to different parts of the world, my information is digestible. I demand a strong field leader from those organizations to disagree with me, so I have a real-time feedback loop. That's been very helpful.

Manage the anti-woke view.

In our training, we start by saying, "There used to be an appetite for DEI because it was the right thing to do." I would tell you a story to make you feel something. Then the meeting would be over, you would reflect 'that's too bad' and go on about your life. "The right thing to do" has a very limited audience. Today, I share it's the profitable thing to do and we now have metrics for that: increase in innovation, less turnover. The training is about building the participant's self-awareness and understanding how they are seen in the organization. It's important because everyone needs to be able to influence. If you don't get on board with this, you're going to lose your effectiveness and influence. We explain the Dunning–Kruger effect, a cognitive bias in which people with limited competence in a particular domain overestimate their abilities. Some researchers also include the opposite effect for high performers: their tendency to underestimate their skills. Imposter syndrome. I have a lot more knowledge than I am leading with. We can marry that or bury that with five or six different topics. Organizations become vulnerable as people become vulnerable.

People want to feel something from their leader.

I was in a prep meeting with a turnaround senior leader coming into the organization. The organization was devastated by the previous leader leaving and being replaced. It was a venture capital group that sent him in, and he offered nothing by way of connection with him. I watched a crisis management team in a half-day take his presentation and humanize him. He was uncomfortable telling stories. Finally, he opened up about his kids. They loved it.

Take steps in your organization to shift out loud.

It may be a three-year journey. You will notice things immediately, be frustrated in six months. In a year, you'll ask if you did the right thing. Then something magical happens in year two. Then in year three, this is who you are. You have to do the hard work and it takes time. You can't have a meeting and it changes. Culture is an emotional reaction to leadership. That means it's not just in the C-suite. It's everyone. Infusion takes time to provide opportunities for leaders and employees to be engaged. The other thing is to teach what will happen without this: *We're going to lose clients, there will be a mass exodus. Younger people won't be attracted to us.* If you don't have this mission reflected on your website, if you have no representation of what they care about, your company won't even get in the game to be able to hire that talent.

I will add to Tracy's point here. From experience, there's an even more sinister danger than capable people not flocking to your company and that's when people don't leave. If the reason employees stay is because they are complacent about change and they are given the opportunity to rest easy in their comfort zone, the organization will end up sitting on a pool of people that are incapable of bringing it to the next level. It's just hard work. Every day, you have to be thinking of the angle you're going to take in fragments, and you must be willing to give things up. Inclusion takes stamina, but the effort is always unquestionably worth it! The saying goes, success begets success. In the case of revealing the real you to manifest your purpose, results are exhilarating and spur you on. Seeing is believing, and bonding.

Let's get back to the real you. What can you do to begin shaping a culture of inclusion? Be purposeful with new joiners in helping them understand what it takes to be successful by sharing your own stories of success and failure. Be open with your team about your vision. Be clear on how you see strategies and projects impacting the company and individuals. Be honest, transparent, and empathetic with others in your organization about what they are doing well and how they can improve. Ask others for feedback and advice. Nothing says to another more strongly that you respect them then by asking for their opinion. Finally, take a stand for positions in which you believe, stand strong in your beliefs yet open to evolving and developing your own thinking beyond the constraints of your own imagination.

Chapter 3
SEEING, BELIEVING, BONDING

"To accomplish great things, we must not only act, but also dream; not only plan, but also believe."

—*Anatole France, journalist*

WHEN I WAS asked to head diversity and inclusion at the premier toy and game company, Hasbro, I was handed the key to the type of leadership role that makes a difference and sets the bright vision for such a storied organization. It started with an exceptionally driven and successful CEO, who believed the organization he was running and the industry in which it operated was frequently inequitable towards women, and he wanted to do something about it. This was in the year of 2015 and A-list actress Ashley Judd had just written an essay in *Variety* detailing how she had been sexually harassed by a then-unnamed media boss in a hotel room. The #MeToo and #TimesUp movements sparked, and with high velocity. The

Chapter 3

voices of survivors were amplified and countless powerful men were held accountable for sexual harassment.

Hasbro's CEO was attuned to these events and the need to recognize and uplift all women in the organization. He supported a robust package of programs for International Women's Day and Women's History Month. The organization had a fair number of women in senior positions within the group, but they were still underrepresented. A lot of these executives came from the technical positions cultivated across the industry, so there simply were not as many women as the field itself is predominantly and historically male oriented.

The CEO's passion for change in this area was very personal. From my diagnosis, perhaps too personal. At the time, he had a seventeen-year-old daughter, and he believed the world was not an equitable place for her. He spoke about this as a motivator. He wanted to use his position to move the needle, which could be effective, but I didn't have a daughter, so what was our common agenda? We rarely spoke of the positive impact a more equitable and inclusive organization could have on the future growth and success of the company. We may have espoused the same values, but for different reasons and end goals from that gap of understanding. This is why allyship must be everyone's agenda.

When I was asked to take a diversity and inclusion role at Moët Hennessy, I first pressed the leader of this organization with a simple question: *What's in it for you and for the company?* The response was that as a company of brands, he did not feel the organization was close enough to the consumer. He also believed the company was not competitive enough in terms of talent to continue to lead in a very dynamic and quickly evolving environment. He was passionate about infusing the organization with new ideas and new ways of thinking about its employees, its partners, and its consumers. I was told I would be able to shape and propel the agenda. It was incredibly motivating to be talking about fundamental change, transformation, and strategic investments to prepare the company for the future and accomplishing that through the lens of a more diverse, equitable and inclusive organization. Having a more diverse and inclusive company leads to more compelling, creative, innovative, profitable ventures. It's simple. We will become dinosaurs if we are not diverse! That is a different mindset. The strategic perspective propels an organization to knowing its consumer with a new level of intimacy. This moves the discussion beyond *a personal sense of inequity*. The former is more long-lasting. When you bring the two together, it's powerful. With both, it lives and breathes in companies through the employees, customers, and partners.

I have had the cherished experience of participating in many business reviews throughout my career where the state of the business is discussed and plans for the future are detailed. In these reviews, there would almost always be an HR component talking about talent, organizational issues, employee morale, and so on, with DEI being somewhat thrown in the haze of the conversation, if mentioned at all. This part of the reviews, otherwise full of data, facts, and figures, rarely felt interactive. However, I must say during my time at Moët Hennessy and specifically during the last two to three years, I cannot remember a business review where leaders were not talking about diversity and inclusion. I consider my initiatives at Hasbro during my tenure there to be a personal failure in terms of embedding and sustaining the tenants of DEI. The progress was marginal and my approach was not strategic. I learned much from that experience, which I have been able to apply to subsequent work in human resources and DEI. Fortunately, since my time there and true to the organization's mission, Hasbro has made great strides across the DEI spectrum in product development, organizational evolution and community engagement. Well-done!

All these early experiences opened my mind to the fact that diversity and inclusion must be foundational and integrated into the strategy of the organization, not just a list of projects and certainly not living solely in the HR strategy and annual planning.

Additionally, we must examine belonging, in particular from the perspective of standing in the shoes of underrepresented people. For example, we can't impress upon women to be more like men and forfeit their uniqueness in order to feel a greater sense of belonging in a male-dominated environment. This would be a prime example of forcing adaptive skills rather than embracing one's legitimate and valuable perspectives. When this is allowed to happen, the result is a suppression of ideas and contributions, along with feelings of isolation and compromised self-worth. Not a productive outcome in any circumstance.

Holidays: A Test of Inclusive Leadership

As I was becoming more grounded in diversity and inclusion as a cornerstone of HR, I became increasingly adept at observing, respecting, and leveraging differences. "Difference" is widespread in both construct and reality. Built In, an online community for startups and tech companies with savvy, relevant thought leadership material, calls out thirty-nine types of diversity in the workplace, ranging from physical abilities, disabilities and cultural backgrounds to age, neurodiversity, language, linguistics, and accents, to name a few. Just think of the variety of lived experiences behind each of these attributes.

I know firsthand we can identify all the colors of the rainbow, but do we appreciate and utilize them individually? Only more recently would there be an increased focus on not only expanding diverse representation but also, taking full advantage of differences. These behaviors move beyond simply managing differences—or worse, tolerating them.

Brimming with enthusiasm at the start of my career, I attended a one-day program touching upon topics such as race, gender, religious orientation, sexuality, and being equitable in everything. A celebration of everyone…in theory. I realized quickly that the training was actually designed around what *not* to say and do as opposed to how one might create a culture of inclusion and belonging. The coaching that dominated the discussion was focused on messaging around the company values. The awareness and subtraction of what might have been construed as offensive language didn't amount to inclusion or celebration at all. No bonds were formed. Suspicion and paranoia that didn't exist before were stirred up by some of the

Chapter 3

coaching. Call it vintage diversity and inclusion. Somewhere in the background it felt like a legal case was being avoided.

In early 2000, I was promoted to be the head of recruitment and diversity for Disneyland in California. I was working in Orlando at the time. This was my first big relocation and career move. New home, new job, new team, new life. I had first visited Disneyland in California with my family as a ten-year-old. As I contemplated this thrilling new role, it seemed unimaginable to be working there, never mind walking the same streets where I never lost the feeling of being a kid on a once-in-a-lifetime family vacation.

It was never quite clear what the mandate was on diversity. Six months later, at Christmas, our recruitment space named "Casting Center" was ready for the holidays and prepared for the rush of applicants who would join the parks and hotels during this peak season. I arrived at work one morning and saw that overnight, a Christmas tree had been erected in the lobby of the waiting area. Fresh off diversity training and attuned to identify and eliminate inequity, I immediately thought, *What about the other holidays?* Shouldn't we represent all of the holidays of the season? I asked some teammates. No one had an answer for this nor had my team been through the same program to which I had earlier been engaged, so the question itself lacked context and relevance for them. Well, my answer was if we're not going to represent all of the holidays, we should not have a Christmas tree. Not everyone is Christian or commercial-Christian during this time of year, so let's not leave anyone out. I understood it was too late to create additional décor for the season, so I had to make a decision.

Without further consultation, I asked to have the tree removed. You know that look in your team's eyes when they are not quite sure if you are joking or if you have completely lost it? I got that look that day. At 8:00 the next morning, someone knocked on my office door to alert me that there was a problem at the Casting Center.

"I think you should come out and see this, Greg," he said ominously.

To set the landscape for the entrance to the Casting Center, it was a heavily-trafficked area. There was a five-story parking garage just across from a narrow promenade where everyone parked and entered the office building. Well, during the morning rush hour, a few employees responsible for décor in the resort were dragging this Christmas tree across the promenade toward a trash container. Intentional or not, they were inelegantly fumbling with glass ornaments, and everyone could hear them scraping across the floor, some dropping off and shattering. It all seemed to happen in the slowest of slow motion as I watched the rush-hour crowd who had stopped with jaws gaping to witness this desecration unfold. I remember thinking, *this was a really bad idea*. After we picked up the pieces, literally and figuratively, I realized that being equitable does not mean everything is the same. We can celebrate one holiday and then do better next year with more or varied celebrations. I did not need to take away the holiday cherished by many to acknowledge the lack of celebration of others. We can admit we're not recognizing everyone instead of taking away from what some people already had. Taking an additive approach is always better. That was a horrifying Greg Grinch-like moment. (hashtag—I never intended to steal Christmas!)

Chapter 3

Keys to Relevance

So many lessons were learned from that singular, dramatic morning.

What is equity? How do you create an environment where people feel included? How do you recognize what is important to the people for whom you are responsible? How do you really listen to people and make sure they are heard? If I had genuinely consulted with the diverse team I had, I could have been saved from making a bad decision. I was given tools and concepts, but I was untrained at implementation. The result was chaos. All voices matter. Not hearing those voices limits our ability to understand other people's perspectives.

Importantly, how we define these concepts are so different than ten or twenty years ago. And how do you prepare for what is to come? Data, eCommerce, artificial intelligence. Five years ago, we didn't have some of these roles in organizations. Simultaneously, we had many positions that have been completely eviscerated thanks to technology that was developed by richly diverse teams somewhere out there. We've moved so far, so fast, in some areas of business and commerce, yet employees can find themselves lonelier and more divided than ever. How can we be more agile in thinking of inclusion? We must be more assertive, more demanding in areas that have been previously overlooked or ignored. This requires taking a stance.

In June 2022, the U.S. Supreme Court overturned Roe v. Wade with its decision in Dobbs v. Jackson Women's Health Organization, which eliminated the federal right to abortion in the United States. Within hours of this reality, many companies went public—some for the first time—about their policies that protect the healthcare provided to women within their organizations. Diversity and inclusion related to one's employees and products is one thing. Taking a stance publicly or against government is quite another.

It comes back to values. If our values include respect for everyone and creating a culture that mirrors this tenant, then we must be able to represent multiple views. Is supporting or not supporting a woman's right to family planning aligned with our values? I would say as a company, if people make the difference, we need to support difference. The company policy may not honor an individual's point of view, but there is still a place for their talent. Then the individual must make the personal choice of working for the company or not. I firmly believe this approach will transcend generations. It is my view that people should find a workplace where they feel respected and recognized, not tolerated.

We spend so much time inside the work sphere where policies either align with our individual lives or not. Think back only twenty-five years ago. It was in 1989 that Denmark became the first country in the world to legally recognize civil unions for same-sex couples. At that time, the notion of companies offering "domestic partner benefits" was progressive, supporting previously neglected employees and their loved ones in unmarried relationships. Over time, similar policies have been adopted around the world, bringing respect, recognition, and dignity along with them.

If we don't have discussions about what is on people's minds, how can we remain relevant? With the ruling of Roe

v. Wade, LVMH released a formal statement within eighteen hours. The organization had been preparing for months following the news leak that this ruling may happen. There was never a great deal of resistance to say the company would support the wellbeing of every employee by providing them with greater access to healthcare and support if needed. Respect and recognition.

Pausing Like a Global Leader

A friend does development work in East Africa. He and his colleagues wrote a great book titled *Listen. Think. Act.: Lessons and Perspectives in Community Development* about the work they facilitated while there. The book is full of the lessons learned over years of development in the region. In reading the book, I picked up a new mantra. Typically when action on any subject is needed, one hears the phrase, "Don't just stand there, do something." However, in their development work, the mantra was, "Don't just stand there, do nothing." Why is this compelling to me? Sometimes, taking immediate action is dangerous. We may impose a solution that is limited by our own personal perspective. Pause. Try to understand what this means to others. Open a dialogue and gain a sense of the visceral emotions that may inform a different solution that will be more successful in the long term. Doing nothing feels frustrating in the moment. but our role as leaders is to facilitate and encourage discussion, to support alternate views and to implement change for the betterment of people and the company.

In a global organization, noticing events, creating dialogue, and forming greater bonds around the greater cause are fundamental in building successful strategies. In tandem, some things are global and are more around standards and structure. I would argue there is infrequently a coherent global solution or strategy to address any particular issues related to diversity, equity, and inclusion. As an example, cultures see race differently. At a company like LVMH with deeply established French roots, leaders must consider the foundational demographics of its heritage, which are a fundamental part of the DNA of most of the seventy-plus brands controlled by the group.

For non-French people working for a French multinational company, leaders need to help them to excel in areas where they have strengths. What did I learn? Like most companies, sometimes we spend too much time imposing our beliefs and our context rather than listening and creating a global framework. So much positive energy sprouts from the grassroots. Can relevance apply to a global framework? Let's explore.

Some will say that diversity is easier in the U.S. and not as applicable in a more homogenous society like Japan. I say it can't come from the same lens. Japan's diversity angle may be generational, or linked to gender, or experience, or language, among other things. Depending upon one's regional or corporate context, the definition of diversity may be limited to specific attributes like skin color or gender, but other cultures and populations may not relate. It is the role of DEI professionals working with management to develop global principles and guidelines around DEI topics, then to empower local leaders to apply those principles within the context of their areas of operation.

Polarization has exploded in recent years to the extent that language and understanding have been hijacked. It makes me wonder if the fringe voices across the world are just better at amplifying their grievances, like a horror movie loaded with jump scares. A *USA Today/IPSOS* poll asked people how they perceived the word *wokeness* and the majority responded positively. According to the poll, "Fifty-six percent of Americans say 'wokeness' encompasses being informed, educated on, and aware of social injustices. In contrast, two in five (39%) say 'wokeness' involves being overly politically correct and policing others' words."

Do we give too much airtime to the loudest voices? Bonding, the very fabric of us as human beings, draws us back to the need to include all voices, not just the loudest who are good at commanding attention. Everyone deserves to be heard, but louder voices don't have greater value, especially in cases where their ultimate goal is to cause disturbance, division, or personal gain.

Bev Jennings, CEO of SEE Company, founded her company to help diversity-forward and inclusion-focused enterprises grow, leading with her vision to 'see everyone elevate'. As former head of global supplier diversity & inclusion at Johnson & Johnson, she's someone to follow. She notes in her book, *See and Believe*, "In being at the forefront of diversity and inclusion, there are outside forces that counter what we see and stand for. It's been eye-opening for me. There are assaults on diversity. A prominent policymaker wants to fight with Mickey Mouse, symbolic of an iconic brand that has endured for a century in bringing creativity, joy, and possibility to billions of people through the generations. Last year, Florida's governor signed legislation that banned public colleges from using tax dollars to implement or promote DEI initiatives. The Florida board of education followed suit, defining DEI as 'programs that categorize individuals based on race or sex for the purpose of differential or preferential treatment'. The education board also said that a 'principles of sociology' course could no longer be taught and would be replaced with a general American history class. closing its office of the chief diversity officer, eliminating DEI positions and administrative appointments, and halting DEI-focused contracts with outside vendors. At the time of the assaults, Disney was making 'Wish', an animated musical-comedy welcoming audiences to the magical kingdom of Rosas, where Asha, an Afro-Hispanic, sharp-witted idealist, makes a wish so powerful that it is answered by a cosmic force—a little ball of boundless energy called Star. Together, Asha and Star confront a most formidable foe—the ruler of Rosas, King Magnifico—to save her community and prove that when the will of one courageous human connects with the magic of the stars, wondrous things can happen."

Using Bev's great illustration of relevant, contrasting events, I also believe it's helpful to analyze what leaders with so much power actually choose to focus on. It depends on the impact they want to make. We assign motives. What is their motive? With all of the shouting, competition, and demonization, sometimes it's hard to know.

Chapter 3

Bev adds, "There will always be the battle between light and darkness. Stay the course emitting your own values, even when the raindrops of discord and disconnect are falling around you."

These words remind me of a personal Thanksgiving ritual. In the early 2000s, living in Paris, my husband, Shawn, and I hosted a Thanksgiving gathering in our apartment, inviting a combination of local and ex-pat friends, some of whom were American and others who had never experienced a traditional American Thanksgiving. In subsequent years, the Americans hosted one night and our French friends hosted another. Even after we moved to Hong Kong, we would travel back to Paris for this occasion. It was a merging of our traditions. A ritual with so much light in the City of Lights. This ritual of connection is so important to me as a bonding experience. We reveled in the sense of community; the uniqueness of culture presented in rituals and food. We will continue to travel far and wide for it.

There will always be voices focusing on the darkness. Seek out the light. Be a positive force on others and you will radiate energy that can create positive change and real impact.

Keys to Connection

Donna Wilson on Multicultural Marketing

Donna Wilson is president of Strategic Intersections ("Where business interests and community needs intersect for mutual benefit"—a perfect sentiment for this book!). Donna has worked for iconic Fortune 100 brands creating transformational strategies and organizational shifts to increase market share. She has advised countless leaders on building global and regional business to maximize sales to diverse consumer markets and designed innovative marketing strategies aligned with ethnicity and cultural characteristics of consumers and clients. Donna leveraged her experience transforming underserved communities by transitioning from community development to a business focus on global DEI introducing strategies to increase representation of women and people of color and retain top diverse talent and build a more inclusive workplace.

Donna is the recipient of "The Economic Justice Award" from The Welfare Law Center and "David Rockefeller Fellow Award" from the Partnership for New York City. She was named in *Crain's New York Business* magazine's "Top 100 Minority Executives" and "Top 40 Under Forty", along with *The Network Journal's* "25 Influential Black Women in Business."

I summarize Donna's range of achievements as one word in all its significance—*connection*.

> Here, she shows the power of threading a culture of connection inside a brand and the possibilities that surround it.

Consumers are empowered, emboldened. Be aware of their needs and include them in your culture.

Going into the banner year, 2000, a lot of companies had multicultural marketing teams and they eliminated them because they wanted to look at consumers as a "total market". After all, shouldn't we all be looking at our customers in a particular way, based on their needs? In theory. But since we're dealing with human beings and unconscious bias, what you're hoping for may never happen. Depending on what your marketing team looks like, you may get a marketer who can only focus on one segment of the population, and you have these disenfranchised segments of the population feeling left out and ignored. Brands, no matter how storied, are only going to get so far. The consumer is changing significantly. It is no longer just the brand. They not only want the product to work for them—they also want the brand to understand their values, their causes. Mass market advertising doesn't speak to everyone. Today, consumers are voting with their dollars, as well as their feet. There has never been a time in history that consumers have been more emboldened and expected more from their companies that provide them with a service. In turn, companies have a choice. They can lean in and understand these needs or do nothing.

If you're choosing to ignore these diverse segments, you're choosing to make a business decision in your market and your company. The numbers are here. The demographics can no longer be ignored; there are large populations of our youth turning voting age every day, graduating from college, starting new jobs in today's work environment, and making decisions for their families. Are these segments of the population you want to ignore? Your future workforce, your future customers, your future patients.

In order to elicit change, you must show business case data and buying power.

I worked for a large company, and our division reported into the top of the house. In my role, I was there to support and develop the global strategy for the consumer business. When anyone saw my résumé, people saw my business background. So many people reached out to me to sit in on their meetings because I had a substantial business acumen. I spent my first several months understanding how the business worked, listening into town halls, and understanding where opportunities were, where business was happening and not happening, then I was able to develop the global DEI strategy. Shortly thereafter, I was approached by a senior leader. The conversation was led by dollars and supported by growth. This leader asked if I would develop a multicultural marketing strategy for their business. I did just that and the strategy was quickly adopted.

Inclusion is a significant part of successful business objectives.

DEI must be embedded into the business strategy first and foremost. It needs to be on the front burner. Once the business opportunities are determined, it is critical to ensure that you have the right talent that has the necessary skills, experience, and capabilities to address the unique needs of the business to produce the necessary outcomes as opposed to wishing and hoping that the peanut-butter approach will work. Inclusion is paramount. Consumers want to know you understand them, value them, and respect their needs as well as their struggles.

> **You don't have to be the founder of a great company to own your part in its legacy.**
>
> Embedding a multicultural marketing strategy that improved the quality of our consumers' lives widened our culture of connection. Simultaneously, in turning the focus inward, I helped to design a sponsorship program for women and people of color because the numbers showed that they were lagging in movement and viewed as very high-potential individuals. Sponsorship is about making sure high performers are moving and developing and getting those opportunities. In order to affect change, we have to take action and be purposeful. That is what has been my commitment in everything that I do.

Donna epitomizes how one person can set up the culture and conditioning for change and make a big impact. I also know firsthand it takes daily effort and momentum, as she points out. In thinking of the brands that I've worked for, I can pinpoint the consequential results of extending a culture of connection to the consumer base. And even though the category of "luxury brands" may seem narrow in terms of target audience, I have seen bonds form from just one well-considered and well-executed partnership or program.

Chapter 4
LUXURY IS IN THE DIVERSITY

"I believe in a passion for inclusion."

—*Lady Gaga, singer-songwriter*

When I joined LVMH in Hong Kong, the company was already on the path to becoming more progressive and energetic champions of DEI. LVMH is a global luxury company composed of more than seventy-five brands and close to 200,000 employees. It is a diverse and complex global organization with deep French heritage and roots. At the time of my joining, my boss was an Asian woman, yet much of the company's top management reflected an older, White, male, French demographic. The management team was ready to bring in different perspectives, more closely reflecting the consumers (thank you, Donna, for underscoring this need!), and what we did as a brand was celebration. Moët Hennessy is a luxury hospitality company, the leading luxury wines and spirits company in the world. Like with Disney, I was able to develop and experiment with strategies and programs. This organization never said "no"; maybe "slow down a bit" but never a *no*. Since my time within LVMH was so focused on developing a culture of DEI, there is a lot of that inspiration in this book. With the support of an inspired leadership team and a mandate to evolve, I knew that working in this organization was going to be fun. There were many crossroads where the implementation of realizing a real culture of inclusion and belonging seemed to be so far off in the future that the inevitable self-doubt arose. We can be so cautious about what we think we want to do, and we're so worried about the values or the judging we might get along the way. Getting out of the mindset of apologizing has been a relief. Having a supportive management team, willing collaborators, and a strong desire to change from many sectors of the organization made the difference.

As this culture was developing and employees and leaders were becoming increasingly more engaged, people started to believe that real change was possible. They felt they could play a role in making the company a better place to work. There is a high level of hospitality in this organization, which is consistent with the diverse wines and spirits portfolio, and teams across the world working with hotels, bars, cruise lines, and other service and celebration outlets. Several years ago, a Pride event was hosted for the first time in the headquarters office. It was a big step, and everyone from that location was invited. The organizing team developed an engaging and interactive event, yet they were understandably nervous about how the event would be viewed. Would people accept such an event in the company's head office? The answer was *yes*. Half of all headquarter-based employees attended, which was a remarkable result for the first Pride event. Essentially, it was Moët Hennessy coming out to itself. A company celebrating its diversity. It was also a monumental statement of the change that was occurring within the culture. This type of inclusion is consistent with who I am: hopeful, welcoming, and solutions driven. Disney had this persona, too. We strived to align who we were in the back of house among our fellow employees with who we were in front of customers.

Another facilitator of this culture is that Moët Hennessy is a luxury company in an industry that is not particularly seen as *luxury*. A bit of humility played to our advantage. When the idea of creating a diversity and inclusion strategy was raised, I deliberately invited a diverse group of employees from around the world to join a team that worked together to develop and deploy the strategy and actions. The team represented the diversity of our employees in generation, gender, orientation, functional role, background, and culture. This diversity was also representative of the company's partners and consumers. I had learned a lesson from my Disneyland Christmas tree experience: Always engage and incorporate a wide variety of voices.

Be real in your actions and act before promoting. Don't just talk about it. If someone is struggling and is not self-aware, do you want to help them? At one point, we weren't doing well in some demographics of representation in the workforce. Evolving a workforce takes time, care, and intention. We worked on how we communicated outside the company. Being on the senior leadership team, my feeling was when we talked

Chapter 4

to candidates, they were much more drawn to an honest, enlightening interview rather than a show. I interviewed someone who later received an employment offer. She shared with me that she had appreciated my honesty about what was "not working". Note that this transparency is a conversation device and strong way to alleviate the imposter syndrome (or feeling like a fraud or phony merely exaggerating our greatness). *We don't have it all figured out, so you (prospective employee) can contribute to solutions!*

In a breakfast interaction with our CEO regarding empowerment, he was talking to the team in Singapore and he was frustrated with repeated concerns raised in town halls and other forums about employees' feelings of "not being allowed to take risks". He probed me, "Where does that come from?" He encouraged people to take risks. I replied that personal narrative would hit home rather than a blanket instruction. "What story do you have about you encouraging your people to take the risk and it failing, and what you did next?" In the next session, he shared a story with the team about the brand taking a big bet in a market on the West Coast of the United States. The investment did not work for a variety of reasons. Team members who attended this town hall and heard this story replayed it to me many times over the succeeding months. They believed in what they heard, and this moment helped to support other initiatives where risk taking was required and where success was not always assured.

As noted in the introduction, *stories* are the way to encourage people to overcome the fear of failure and know that they can leap forward. From a company perspective and on a micro level, it's more about the learning than the actual failure or success. Failure is important to a company that is growing, and learning from it creates a sense of empowerment. The sidelines are wider, and if things don't work out, we still find success in knowing that we tried and can share insights on what was learned. This goes against people's natural competitive nature where the spotlight is on "success". Management should foster this storytelling and not with the throughline of "Don't do that because it didn't work five years ago."

I raise this point and share this story to highlight something I often hear. When it comes to inclusion and belonging, individuals are often concerned about doing or saying the "wrong thing" however they define the "wrong thing". This may include misrepresenting someone's name, culture, gender, etc. It could be a fear of using non-inclusive language or exhibiting dominant behaviors that may have been successful in the past yet are no longer appreciated or serve the greater good, especially in increasingly diverse teams and organizations. The greater good is derived by being open and transparent about your limitations. Let me share an example.

In my role as the head of people and organization at Gay Games Hong Kong, I had the rare opportunity to be engaged with a wide cross-section of Hong Kong society. Many sectors of society had a vested interest in seeing a successful event. The leadership team of Hong Kong Gay Games endeavored to create the most welcoming and inclusive event possible. One effort we launched was inviting a number of individuals to participate in a Gender Inclusion Advisory Committee. This group represented a rainbow of identities across the gender

Chapter 4

spectrum and as our first organizing meeting kicked off, I was very nervous about doing or saying the wrong thing. We really needed this group to help us, and alienating an individual or group could have resulted in very negative consequences. Positively engaging them would provide us with access to a wide spectrum of views in an area where most of us were deeply lacking in knowledge. It was important for us to navigate the pitfalls of language. Before the meeting, I did my research and tried as best as I could to prepare to engage the group. I realized there was no way I could fully equip myself to avoid using non-inclusive language. I just did not know enough, and even to me it felt like the appropriate language regarding gender inclusion was changing by the day. I decided to kick off the meeting by highlighting how important his gathering was, how critical their voices were to our effort, and I asked them in advance for their patience in helping me and the organization to learn. I explained that I was almost certain to miss the most inclusive language, yet that was the point of why their input was so important. The kickoff went well, as did the subsequent engagement of this group, which was significant. Following the kickoff meeting, several members of the group approached me and shared their appreciation for the humility in which we started our engagement and how much they appreciated my words, transparently sharing that I looked to them for help. I certainly misspoke a few times in that meeting, yet always with positive intent. When we approach these types of discussions with transparency and positive intent, we can reduce the anxiety of saying or doing the "wrong thing" and even more importantly, we can open ourselves to learning from others by giving them a voice.

Keys to Inclusion
Lady Gaga's Cause and Effect

It sounded like an advertisement, and it was: "Today, more than ever, the world needs the power of creative freedom. A force to open up new horizons, to move us forward. A force that brings Lady Gaga and Dom Pérignon champagne together for a collaboration. This is the celebration of how pushing boundaries of creation, constant reinvention, and passionate dedication to one's craft can elevate us, individually and collectively."

The partnership brought all the bling you can imagine, including limited-edition bottles and a sculpture designed by Lady Gaga herself. For these significant collaborations, Dom Pérignon wholeheartedly embraces the preferred causes of the artists, and in this case, the alliance brought forth meaningful support for Lady Gaga's Born This Way Foundation. This foundation is a dream for expressing the need for bonds and securing them early, since their focus is on youth.

Born This Way Foundation leverages innovative programming and partnerships to model, convene, and support healthy conversations about mental wellness, to connect youth with resources and services that support their mental health—online and offline—and to encourage and build communities that understand and prioritize mental and emotional wellness.

To bring their impact into perspective, this is a snapshot of accomplishments in 2023 alone:

- 80K+ participants trained in teen Mental Health First Aid
- 10K+ participants achieved the Be There Certificate
- 291M+ acts of kindness pledged
- 48K+ surveyed for research
- 1,630+ mental health-focused projects for classrooms funded
- 600+ nonprofits supported
- US$3M+ donated to nonprofit partners
- 200+ service events organized

Bling meets the power of belonging!

Cool Hunting wrote of the collaboration, "At a time when celebrity wine and spirits endorsements are more commonplace than ever, it's clear from Gaga's body of work with Dom Pérignon (and her passion and earnestness in speaking with us about it) that, again, this is no ordinary brand partnership. 'To be frank with you,' she continued, 'I know that a lot of artists or celebrities work with brands and do collaborations, but for me, it's really important that I work authentically with people. It's just the way that I am. I can't do it any other way.'"

I love this story because the participants, the project, and the context align. Let me explain how this iconic brand activation and the growing internal culture of inclusion come together to create a truly memorable moment. Across Asia Pacific, teams were kicking off a variety of initiatives to support the company's recently energized focus on becoming more innovative and consumer relevant by being more diverse and inclusive. The initiatives were done at the pace and within the context of the different locations around the region, an incredibly culturally diverse part of the world. The image from the West is often that Asia is one homogenous culture or location. Country to country, the cultures across this vast region vary significantly in terms of their richness, heritage, and deep roots.

At the same time, one team in the region, based in a multicultural Muslim and traditional society, began a series of women's empowerment events. In this culture, women played a strong role but often, not a leading role. In the first session, three women representing different predominant cultures withing the country talked about their experiences. During one of these sessions, a participant bravely raised the issue of identifying as LGBT at work and at home. When this was raised, some of the employees felt uncomfortable and suggested that the subject of LGBT was not appropriate for discussion. The topic was changed, but the door to dialogue had been opened, slowly and respectfully. This was progress.

A follow-up session on women empowerment was conducted and once again, the subject of LGBT was raised and this time, a further discussion ensued about how to value and include LGBT members in society. Perhaps someone in the audience, or any number of people, identified as LGBT. Days following that second session, an email from the marketing manager who handled the Lady Gaga partnership announced, "The queen of pop music is aligned with the queen of champagne!" As was her responsibility, she shared all of the creative assets that had been developed to promote the partnership and at the end of her email, she wrote, "As an LGBT person, this partnership is extremely important to me...and why I am so proud to work here."

She came out to all of her colleagues in that email and she received an outpouring of support. We had a conversation, and she said, "Friends in the office know I'm gay and it's like a family in our office; I wanted to share this with the broader organization." What I learned from her manager was telling. He told me he was not aware of the employee's orientation nor that she had planned that very brave communication, yet he commented that he had never seen her do better work. This was a powerful story of engagement and empowerment and how leaders and colleagues can create safe spaces for employees to thrive.

The impact of Malaysian actress Michelle Yeoh winning an Oscar for her role in the film, "Everything Everywhere All at Once", was epic. You could not contain the excitement among my colleagues around her first-of-a-kind representation of them on such a grand stage. As with my colleague, this talented, glamourous woman made those who identified with her very proud, and she opened doors for others to be courageous in their own pursuits.

These are just a couple of examples of how the parts fit and align with who we are when we feel seen among a broader, diverse base. We bond more openly and freely. There is something to be said about star power, of course, because they have the gargantuan platforms for any theme or value they want to portray, but they're also imperfectly perfect humans. They show us the way. When brands follow suit and are more purposeful about talent and making sure it's diverse, representative, and inclusive, we all hold the keys to connection and inclusion.

Chapter 5
CEILINGS ARE MADE OF BAMBOO, TOO

"Who you follow matters. I am motivated by others who overtly proclaim accountability."

—*Enrico Biscaro, global executive and consultant*

AT THE INCEPTION of this book-writing process, a grim diversity and inclusion report came out furiously shouting that US$8 billion on said private and public programs in the U.S. had missed the mark. In so many words, the gaping hole appeared to be social connection, which can't be overemphasized these days. Thus, if I may say, part of the reason I felt compelled to write this book.

At that same time I was digesting the news of the US$8 billion deficit, I was proud to have been in the midst of launching a truly innovative program across the Moët Hennessy business in Asia.

Chapter 5

We embarked on creating an Asia Leadership Acceleration program, with a renowned consultant from well-recognized organizational effectiveness partner, Third Opinion Partners. We had been talking for years about the barriers that East Asian leaders had in attaining the most senior leadership positions in multinational companies. Across the Fortune 50 landscape, to date, there are no East Asian CEOs. While East Asian leaders are successful across Asia and lead some of the world's largest companies, these leaders have yet to make their mark in the world of Western-based, multinational Fortune 50 companies. As the importance of the business and consumer across East Asia becomes an ever more critical key to the success of multinational companies, it was more than a curiosity to note the lack of representation at the top of these companies.

Our consultant pulled 360-degree leadership assessment reviews from different parts of the world that had been conducted over the prior twenty years. What he found was that the participating East Asian leaders had rated themselves lower in confidence, speaking up, and presence in meetings in six out of ten self-rating dimensions. In Western companies, these behaviors often make or break one's career. If you don't have presence and you fail to represent your point of view, you don't get noticed. During my seventeen years working in Hong Kong and Mainland China, I often heard the notion that people in Hong Kong are really quiet; they don't have an opinion. This was partially driven by the experience of being on conference calls where most of the Americans or Europeans were working in a strong first or second language, English. Many participants representing Asia were also disadvantaged by educational systems that taught them to speak only when spoken to. Also, global calls usually take place during late-night hours in Asia and normal business hours in Europe and the U.S. When you are raised through a system that believes anything short of perfect is failure, then you find yourself in a room with a collection of people who run a global organization, it is intimidating, to say the least. It goes without saying that this can be a barrier to speaking up, especially when you may hold an opposing viewpoint. We refer to this as "the bamboo ceiling". These are the systemic barriers to advancement that suppress these brilliant talents and give others the impression that they don't have opinions, or they do not care to be heard. The program we developed focused on two aspects:

(1) being prepared to manage how they represented themselves, and

(2) developing sponsorship for careers at senior levels.

The closer you are to the center, the more sponsorship you have. If you're thousands of miles away and you're not at the water cooler or clinking glasses at the end of the day, you miss the moments of familiarity that can be important in creating sponsorship and opportunity. As much as we would like to say there is equity in talent management, proximity and familiarity are extremely strong influences that must not be overlooked.

Cultural context is essential and more important than ever. As such, for this groundbreaking, bamboo ceiling-shattering program, we selected the first group of delegates, the cohort, to take three days of business case and behavioral skilling in Singapore, then we flew them to Paris. We trained the sponsors as well. This was fieldwork in all senses. We curated a group that had advantages in this area, commercial functions, and the gap between them and success was not that far away.

The sponsors included the CEO, the global commercial leader, two heads of the largest brands, the head of human resources, and the head of talent management, among others. I spell out the roles here because success of the program was also dependent on the visibility and buy-in of the most senior management. While the primary focus of the program was elevation of the profiles in Asia, the same principle and method could be applied to any underrepresented and under-recognized demographic, from anywhere within the business. I also started to recognize hints of other organizations doing this. (And it's okay to copy. Let's spread the bonds!) Our objective was to have more Asian people running the Asian businesses and more Asian people in senior global positions. If we didn't make dedicated efforts to break this ceiling, we would just keep recording and discussing the same statistics of underrepresentation.

The development of senior leadership is a long-term investment, so while we will not know for several years if the mission of developing Asian leaders for global leadership roles was successful, we definitely learned a few important things. First, it is essential to reinforce that the program is not meant to change people. We did not set out to make Asian talents more like their Western colleagues. The objective was to acknowledge the cultural and behavioral differences and take advantage of them, highlighting individual strengths and giving individuals tools to fully leverage their talents. Second, sponsorship is key. Senior leadership familiarity and support will contribute to the future success and promotion and these individuals. Finally, any intense development experience such as this one can highlight both *potential* and *limitations*, and this initiative did just that. Breaking the bamboo ceiling will not happen overnight, yet it can be achieved with purposeful focus and action. Let's watch these talents fly!

The bamboo ceiling program was a long time in the making. As with any worthwhile change initiative, early iterations had been discussed for years with my consulting colleague. The program had to be timed to align with strategic priorities. It was an important element to build rapport and understanding. This could not be a remote program—especially for the first intake—so it didn't help that COVID-19 officially delayed it for two years, but the team was dedicated to the cause, and we kept pressing.

For further context, I was invited to a charity event in London hosted by D&I in Grocery, an organization in the UK with a community of ninety-plus partners focused on driving change through shared learning and mentoring. They have a robust agenda around D&I, including providing support to local communities during COVID-19 as people struggled to get food. They hosted a festive Christmas concert in a gothic church (think cold!). I was sitting in the loft of this historic church observing the audience below. Many of the grocers are from family-owned businesses, some dating back generations. To them, diversity is their livelihood, as represented by their employees and their clientele. The D&I in Grocery Program was created for the industry by the industry, offering sponsorship opportunities for owners, employees, mentors, and mentees alike. Their programs create bonds and understanding that help participants navigate their own D&I landscapes. To help the underrepresented employee develop the tricks and tactics needed to thrive in an organization. How do these organizations of all sizes stay relevant to and reflective of their consumers and employees? How do you make sure the sales team is reflective? The bar owner? The restaurant? It comes from appreciating the differences across the spectrum of teams and markets, and by going beyond accepting the differences but taking advantage of them.

We can become fixated on old beliefs, old images and perceptions that keep us safe, but these can be barriers to change. It's not easy to change. You could be on an airplane where half of the passengers are only comfortable with male pilots. Would they be happy about female pilots being denied the same training and employment opportunities as men? Do they not want to see aspiring female pilots realize their career aspirations? Does it matter? By nature, I am a very hopeful person. It can be tiring because we keep running into the same barriers over and over. Systems work against underrepresented people. Political structures work against underrepresented people. Oftentimes, people work against underrepresented people. As much as we strive to influence ways of thinking and acting, systems are well-established and they take much longer to alter.

For one of these programs, I was with the Asia Pacific human resources team in Vietnam, and because of COVID-19, this was the first time I had been with everyone in person for more than two years. A facilitator helped us through the first two days. I realized that a lot of change was needed yet in the team-building and planning phases. What was remarkable in the last day and moments is when we were standing in a circle talking about our feelings of being together, of bonding. Most of these team members were the sole human resources manager in their respective country, so I was conscious of trying to build connection between them. I was proud of them because they were such a strong group of collegial and supportive people. It was immensely rewarding to have these moments with them. I was so exhilarated and exhausted! Leaders: It's okay to say! Thinking and musing and reprocessing and refiling is exhausting. Physically, you can power through with naps and sleep, sleep on the plane on the way back, but mentally, you must be a present, engaged, inclusive leader.

When I was refreshed after that weeklong excursion, I remember my high level of exhilaration and engagement. The travel, the achievements can all amount to an addiction, but you need a recharge. I had thirty one-on-one meetings during that week and tried to absorb it all.

I remember talking about my husband, Shawn, and it was easy for one of the managers with whom I was speaking to ask me a question about him without hesitation or discomfort. That is different than when I joined. I vividly recall those moments when I was first meeting my colleagues and the repeated questions of, "Do you have a family?" I would reply that my family was with me in Hong Kong. The next question was more often than not, "What does your wife do?" Stand in the shoes of both the questioner and the questioned in this situation. The questioner feels uncomfortable that they have made a mistake or worse, an insult. The person being asked the question has to reply to new colleagues, people who are only being introduced for the first time, by coming out and trying to make the questioner feel less awkward about the question. Patience and understanding are the best remedies and are likely to create even stronger bonds of trust and connection in such situations.

In the bamboo ceiling program, the consultant drilled us for our own answer to: Why is diversity and inclusion so successful in some companies and not in others? I can speak from the experience in three companies. When we started with the agenda that D&I would be a foundation of transforming the company, then it worked. If we started the agenda with "there will be more justice and equity in the company", it did not work. While those are hopefully outcomes, they are not necessarily going to drive structural or strategic change in an organization that will then live on its own and become more diverse and equitable. Whatever diversity's objective is oftentimes very clear. The definitions of "equity" and "justice" are very individual. I would have to figure out this equation 8,000 times. This is where we get hung up in the craft—we can't be everything to everybody. What are we trying to accomplish with the diversity or inclusion agenda? The chief diversity officer is trying to make progress but can easily be pulled into too many agendas.

Inclusive leadership is just good leadership; it's not separate and distinct. Every program should be designed with inclusion in mind, not as a sideline but as core to the program and its outcomes. Being mindful and inclusive in interviews is just good interviewing. When this is done, the system works, and the outcome is diverse and inclusive, and the company ends up with better teams who are more engaged because they feel like they belong.

I've learned that a company should strive for creating a culture that accounts for access, sponsorship, and opportunity for everyone. Employee resources groups (ERGs) will run their course and their impact will ebb and flow as progress is made and lost. At Disney, it was incredible to see ERGs for women, LGBT, and Latino employees in the late 1990s. Back then, these groups were made up of passionate, committed, underrepresented people sharing ideas and grievances with each other. Although this helped in creating a sense of inclusion and bonding, it may not have had a significant impact on driving the systemic change within the overall organization. Twenty-five years later, the most successful ERGs of today are aligned with the corporate and people strategies, supporting not only internal progress but also, advising the company on the markets in which they operate, growing links to the community and enhancing the company image and attractiveness, commercially and as employers.

Chapter 6

DISCOVERIES OF A LIFELONG LEARNER

"After all these years, I am still involved in the process of self-discovery. It's better to explore life and make mistakes than to play it safe. Mistakes are part of the dues one pays for a full life."

—*Sophia Loren, film star*

IN HER LATE twenties, unbound by a recently broken pre-marital engagement, my mother learned about a teaching job with an American oil company in Saudi Arabia. It was 1958, and she signed a two-year contract. She set out from New York and flew on a propeller plane to Boston, then to Gander in Canada, on to Amsterdam, to Rome, to Cairo, and finally to Dharan, Saudi Arabia. That's a long way! She was going to earn twice what she could make teaching at home, and live in company-supplied housing on what was an American compound halfway around the world.

Chapter 6

Mom was only the second Western woman ever to go into the harem of the king of Saudi Arabia, individually selected to share Western teaching methods for gifted children.

She taught English for two years, during which time she met her fiancé, another American on an overseas contract. They planned to marry when they both returned home. In preparation for their marriage, he returned to New York before her. On her way home, she decided to make it a six-month journey throughout the Middle East, India and Asia where she reveled in the cultural immersion, amassing a treasure trove of interesting stories and experiences that would be recounted for the rest of her full life. Among those stories were encounters she had with interesting people along the way. She met celebrated author W. Somerset Maugham in the lobby bar of one of the Oriental Hotels in Singapore. Years before his disappearance, she met "Thai Silk King" Jim Thompson in a similar setting. There weren't many young, attractive, Western women traveling solo in this part of the world, so it's safe to assume she attracted some attention! Then she arrived in Hong Kong, where she decided to have a custom wedding dress made for the big day that awaited her upon arriving home. While waiting for the dress to be completed, Mom received a late-night call at her hotel informing her that her husband-to-be had been shot and killed. He was an innocent bystander in a random shooting at the Carlyle Hotel in New York City. Her travel adventures were cut short, and she returned home to pick up the pieces of her life. Shortly thereafter, she met the man who would later become my father.

In many ways, my mother created the mold for the way I have lived my life over the past thirty years. I have traveled, studied, and worked abroad. I have always been drawn to new experiences in different places. Traveling enhances your cognitive abilities, creativity, resilience, confidence, personal growth, and understanding around numerous topics. Throughout our twenty-five-year relationship, Shawn and I have lived this adventure. It's a unique life, and fortunately, we both share the same appreciation for exploration and new challenges. Had we not, our life together would have been very different. Our work life is woven into each other's. We both love what we do.

Blending and Bonding

I never want to put words in Shawn's mouth because the blend of our perspectives has always brought us closer and given us the ability to overcome many challenges. His words here illustrate the power of my strongest bond in life, but they also speak to how I aspire every day to be an inclusive leader and colleague. How he describes our experiences together makes me want to stay committed to creating cultures of connection.

In Shawn's words, "I would not be as successful in my career had it not been alongside Greg. I would not have had the courage or the confidence to work abroad. I had never traveled to Europe before visiting Paris with Greg in early 2001. He had a business trip and I tagged along. In August of the same year, we sold our houses and cars and we moved there. My parents had never been to Europe before visiting us in Paris. Until 2005, I had never traveled to Asia. Greg traveled to Hong Kong on a business trip in June of that year and by November, we were living there. I had never set out to live and work abroad. Opportunities came along. We've supported each other. There were times when I wasn't working, but Greg was; and vice versa. It was always okay because we had each other, and we had some balance. Greg has given me confidence to learn, develop and to take calculated risks. At Disney, before I met Greg, my manager was hiring for a position and interviewed several candidates. There were two of us she really liked, and she couldn't decide between us. Somehow, she got approval to hire both of us by creating another role. One day, while the three of us were driving back to the office in her car, she asked us the same question: How far do you want to go within Disney? I had never thought about it, but my answer was immediate. I said I want to go as far as possible where I can still have balance in my life, and I won't know that level until I get there. At that moment, I really didn't know how far my career would advance, but I was confident that life would tell me 'that's enough'. Today, I can say I've gone further than I ever expected, but only because Greg and I have done it together."

I concur. I wouldn't have had the confidence to pick up and move around the world without Shawn, who's always the conscience for me, from simple things like rereading an email before I send it, to more complicated things like listening to my talking points before I have a difficult discussion with someone. Or going in to talk to my boss to negotiate something—how should that go? Those are all things that if I take my own way of approaching things and I marry it with Shawn's, then it's a pretty complete way to be successful. We have complementary skills, which has helped us. In many ways, it is the byproduct of how we were raised. We are each diverse in our own ways but we share the same value system, which has created a bond that we can always rely upon.

Life is not perfect. We all have problems in our jobs, relationships, family—life in general. I like therapy powerhouse The Fibus Group's description of the *marital bond*: "a unique connection that only a couple can share. It provides support, safety, understanding, and love to each member of the couple. Although the marital bond is one all-encompassing description of a marriage, relationships have many aspects that make up a solid foundation. The key aspects that make up the marital bond are respect, trust, and intimacy."

Our first international move together was in August 2001, less than two years after we met while both working at Walt Disney World in Orlando, Florida. Such a move required an unbridled amount of trust, respect, and intimacy, to be sure. I had moved from Orlando to Los Angeles eighteen months earlier to lead recruitment for Disney's California Adventure Park. After an extended long-distance relationship, we decided we would live together in California. Shawn sold his house, arranged a moving company, interviewed for jobs, and mentally prepared to leave his home of twelve years to start our life together. Just before his relocation, I was asked to go to Paris for three months to fill in for my friend and respected HR colleague, Jo Lamb, who had to step away from the role due to sick leave. Shawn canceled his moving company, put all his belongings into a storage unit and the two of us flew to Paris

Chapter 6

(each with two suitcases filled with clothing and essentials, plus two dogs) for what we thought would be a temporary excursion before settling down in California. Three months turned into four years living in Paris.

Not everything was glamorous and beautiful about living in France. On a basic level, we didn't speak the language and the winter months were cold, dark, and wet, unlike the balmy climates we had left behind in Florida and California. On a more complex level, the culture was a shock to our systems. Protests and debates were commonplace. We had lost our community, our sense of belonging. It was more difficult than we expected to forge close friendships, but once developed, those relationships became deep, meaningful, and lifelong.

Not knowing how long our European adventure would last, we became obsessed with visiting new countries and Paris was the perfect hub for short getaways, commonly referred to as *séjours* in France. Our travel map on the wall collected a few new pins every month. We loved having the opportunity to experience the diversity of Europe in small, bite-sized doses, and we loved doing it together. We imagined what it would be like to do the same thing in Asia. To find ourselves a hub, then live, travel, and experience new cultures just like we had done in Europe. Shawn had never been to Asia, but we decided together that that's what we wanted to do, and we started plotting our exit strategy from France.

Blessed with fortuitous timing once again, Disney asked me in May of 2005 to travel to Hong Kong to support the pre-opening of Hong Kong Disneyland. It was meant to be a brief assignment of four months, but we knew if I played my cards correctly, this could be our ticket to Asia. As I left Paris bound for Hong Kong, Shawn said, "Don't screw it up!".

Shawn picks up the story from here. It's only fair!

"We were at my sister's wedding in Jamaica, relaxing on lawn chairs at the beach when Greg's boss called. I could only hear half of the conversation, but I knew what he was asking Greg to do. I also knew that if Greg went to Hong Kong and proved himself, they would not want him to leave. I remember turning to my parents and saying, 'Greg is going to Hong Kong for a short project and hopefully we can move there.' My mother replied, 'Well you're never going to see me there because I'm not traveling that far!' Had I not experienced the ups and downs of living in Paris over the four years prior, that probably would have been my response, too."

Shawn continues, "I never would have moved to Asia by myself. Like a lot of steps throughout our life together, we're committed to the decision, but we're not locked into the outcome. If circumstances change, we discuss and make the next decision together. That's an important part of our bond. 'Let's go to Paris' turned into four years. 'Let's go to Hong Kong' turned into seventeen." Incidentally, my parents visited us in Hong Kong two years after we moved there."

Making Sense of Cultural Differences

We don't have a button to push for downloading and assessing all the knowledge and experiences we've amassed in our lifetime. But when it comes to our self-awareness and how we treat others in the lens of cultural sensitivities, it's good to have tests and tools to help us discern.

My team and I completed the Intercultural Development Inventory® (IDI®), a theory-based, developmental psychometric instrument grounded in a comprehensive, cross-culturally validated theory of intercultural competence. A mouthful, I know, but what's important is that the IDI measures both one's mindset and skillset, which allows individuals and groups to better understand successes and challenges related to their intercultural interactions. I wanted to have a wakeup discussion about where we were in the measurement of D&I.

Once the results were in, we built a three-hour experience for the top thirty executives in the company. People tend to overrate themselves in cultural competency. It is normal. Self-rating is often higher than the reality. I'm relatively high on the scale, having lived and worked abroad for over twenty years, and because I have developed my own curiosity and skills in managing across differences. I am constantly seeking perspectives beyond my own bubble—talking to Uber drivers and learning tidbits about their lives, reading a book about another culture, or mentoring students; generally being curious about others, especially those outside of my usual crowd. This takes work. My upbringing provided me with the grounding for becoming acquainted with the world and I've been fortunate enough to have a life partner who embodied this quest with me. But how does one continue to move up the scale? How much more intercultural experience can you have in your life? Guest expert Harland Chun could be a role model for us all.

Keys to Inclusion

Harland Chun On Leadership Cultures

My friend and former boss and colleague at Hasbro, Harland Chun, works with multinational clients, consulting and coaching their senior leaders and leadership teams to develop self-awareness and engagement skills to maximize their contribution and exploit imminent career advancement opportunities. If he is involved, you can guarantee increased cultural understanding of working with managers across global markets, international field leaders' communication and navigational skills. His experience in diverse leadership roles in global companies enables Harland to always coach and mentor in the "right" context. This skillset is hard to find, and here, he hands us the keys to his rare insights.

Look at your unique lived experience in a cultural context.

I was born in Hong Kong and my family immigrated to America when I was thirteen. My dad went to a boarding school outside of Boston and when we looked at his yearbook, he told me, "You're going to school here." So, I went—and I had to repeat a year because my English was not good enough.

Fast-forward, with a command of English, I wanted to teach so I signed up for a program at Yale teaching in China. Hong Kong was a very capitalistic city and I realized teaching was probably not my bag. I had too much energy and a keen interest in business, so I ended up hooking up with a family friend who owned a business spanning Asia and distributing American product brands. I shadowed him, and that is how I got started in business.

All my life, I've been in international consumer brands starting with Foster Grant when I moved back to the US working out of New York and then Reebok. I spent sixteen years at the Reebok headquarters managing the Latin America business. Eventually I went out to manage their business in Japan and to a startup joint venture in China. In 2006, a German company, Adidas, acquired Reebok. I was one of sixteen executives put on the integration planning team. After six months, I realized I would never survive in that German culture. At the age of fifty-one, I struck out because I wanted to try my hands outside. That's when I ended up at Hasbro. I ran their business in Asia Pacific working out of Singapore. I was asked to coach executives because of my background of working in different geographical regions. Then I began my executive coaching career at Linkage.

Never stop noticing the lack of diversity in the room just because there is comfort in the room.

I always think about corporate culture as a very important part of culture. For example, in one company where I worked for sixteen years, I had thirteen bosses including eight presidents. The founder was a visionary, had great ideas but was not a very structured guy. One of the reasons for our successes is we were like a Jeep; the direction may be north, but sometimes we go east, west, and then we would take a little U-turn and end up still going north. That drove people who came in from competing brands crazy. They were very structured. At dinner, sitting next to the head of global HR, I said, "Tell me about the brand."

He said, "People come to a meeting thinking they're going to be heard in what they propose but most of the decisions have already been made. At the previous company I worked for, it was the total opposite. All ideas, passion, everything went. Everyone was heard.

One of my close colleagues, a Black woman, and I were having lunch at the German headquarters. She said, "Look around you. There's not a shade of color." I looked around and sure enough, everyone had blond hair, blue eyes. They were German and French. In the Asia-Pacific business, there was not one Asian executive, so I thought, *Harland, how long do you think you're going to survive in this environment?* That was a wakeup call. I was a Chinese guy with poor Spanish running the Latin America business. I was capable of leading, so they let me lead.

My counterpart was a Frenchman. In those days, I would receive texts on my Blackberry with comments like, "You shouldn't have said that." All for political reasons, which I did not want to navigate.

You don't have to be a regional cultural expert to be able to read the room.

In distribution, I always knew the differences between a principal, a brand owner, and a distributor. I learned to understand their individual sensitivities and interests. If I was not representing them in front of the global product or marketing meetings, even though they were the smallest region, my partners would not hesitate to pick up the phone and call the founder because of their own multimillion-dollar enterprises. They would not hesitate to go past me in order to vocalize their point of view. So, I had to make sure I was always representing my constituents while at the same time, always being fair to the company.

When my Argentinian JV partner, who speaks very little English, leaves me a forty-minute voicemail, I have to listen to it a few times. His knowledge is helping me represent my constituents. If you have a seat at the table, I don't care what color or gender you are, imagine you have all these constituents in a glass window behind you who say, "Are you representing us, all the things we've talked about, in front of your bosses?"

Know your team as individuals and as workers.

My door was always open. As a result, anyone dropped in to have a conversation. Getting to know people one-on-one has its merit. "What's your story? Tell me about your background." That's one of the ways I find is successful in establishing relationships with people.

Determine how personal culture can work with company culture. Find soft spots where the person can fit and make a difference.

When I'm working internationally, I always make fun of Australians, French, and Brits. They have no fear of speaking up. And Indians? "If you don't understand my English because of my accent, that's your problem." Latins, Asians are not heard as strongly or as clearly because of accents and "not expressing themselves well." That is what I've witnessed working with multinational groups. Last year, I coached sixteen VPs and above from a U.S. consumer bank. No white males. All underrepresented groups including white females. Common themes came up: aversion to self-promotion and networking.

We ended up spending an extra session on self-promotion. Indulge me. Why is it significant to exercise your voice? You have a seat at the table, and you need to use it. You now have to think like the table, but without sacrificing your authenticity. What is your personal brand? What does the brand stand for? What are your brand attributes? Don't wait for someone else to promote your brand. You have to define what kind of leader you want to be. Understand your life story and its importance to your brand and to your purpose. Share your story in a vulnerable way and show yourself. Represent your cause and constituency with conviction, expertise, and experience. Imagine your team is in the back of the room watching how you articulate your position. How do you become assertive in your own style? You're already promoted. It's about maintenance and preserving your position now. You already made the team. Don't you want to go and play? It's what you're being paid to do. Senior leadership doesn't know what you stand for. Worse, they think you don't want to engage. This is how other people look at you if you don't speak up.

Practice empathy to get the results you want for yourself and others.

I'll give you an example of a Black woman executive that I work with. I think the world of her. She's in her early forties. A doer. An SVP in this financial institution. Based on a 360, you can tell she's an achiever and everyone goes to her for problem solving. She asked me, "Why am I always the person that my former bosses, who are all White, come to when they hire new people, all White, to train them, instead of giving me those opportunities?" Her other statement was, "My boss, who is a White male, always wants to avoid racial and gender issues. He's in his forties." I said, "You need to have honest conversations. It's sensitive and awkward, but ask outright why he's sending these people to you and why you aren't considered for these strategic roles? Maybe they haven't thought about it. If people are truly not biased in any way, they simply may have seen you as so niche and as a doer, but never thought of it the way you think. For your immediate manager, it's a bloody shame for someone in their early forties trying to avoid racial and gender issues. I know nothing about growing up African American, little about growing up white in the South, so if I had the opportunity to work with people coming from these diverse backgrounds, I would love to have those honest conversations with them."

A woman I coached for three years and got promoted during that time told me years later after people left in droves that there were issues with being a woman at this workplace. I was always so proud of having more women direct reports than other regions. You would think the consensus was "Oh, Harland must be sensitive to this gender issue," but I had no clue that was going on in the headquarters and how the women executives were feeling.

If you don't understand the other side—a different country, race, gender—if you don't know how the other person is thinking, it's really difficult to be an effective leader for all.

Listen and be emotionally present without bias.

We're living in a divisive society. Essential traits at this time would be *adaptiveness*, *open-mindedness*, and *positivity*. In this kind of environment, we need to have a heart, compassion, show we care about the business and the people with active "listening with intent", in coach speak. Listening while trying to grow and understand is more important than ever. As a coach, it's my job to make people more self-aware. Outreach efforts have to be more intentional now more than ever. That motto of cross-functional and cross-cultural is imperative. In whatever we try to do, accept less and give more. Who are the givers? Takers? Make yourself feel uncomfortable while making others comfortable. It's not easy talking about gender, race.

Everyone has a story. I did an online course, and one of the disciplines was offline, dividing into groups to discuss leadership journeys and to tell their stories. That is one of the most effective exercises. It's up to us to craft that story to make it interesting to other people. We learn from each other's stories. No matter where you're working in the world, you need to be able to connect and engage with composure. Most importantly, you have to overcome self-prescribed restraints like "not doing self-promotion", accent, shyness. Pay attention and understand nuances. Smile and give more! These actions are understood everywhere in the world.

Chapter 7
LOVELY TO HEAR

"All leaders can and should utilize empathy and life experiences to build while continuously improving their work relationships. We have had the same paradigm of work and leadership for so long, but now we know you do not have to show up at an office to be a strong leader. You do not have to keep everything bottled up inside. You do not have to hold all the answers."

—*Paul Wolfe,* author of Human Beings First

IF ONE THING has become clear in my leadership journey, it's that I want to understand the perspective of all people. A trusted colleague once told me, "You're the perfect bridge between this movement of DEI and what seems safe to digest, which is a White, Western guy. I'm not threatened by you even though you're going to challenge my thinking." We're all perfectly aware of our height and eye color, aren't we? Sometimes, I wish there was a way for our heart and our

Chapter 7

potential to be more pronounced like these characteristics we present in an instant. At the same time, I don't personally have any issues with being a White, Western guy! Stigma, preconceived notions, assumptions, and bias come from the outside—and every single one of us has been the subject of this at one time or another.

During the summer after George Floyd's murder in May 2020 while in police custody, a group of high school classmates—around forty of us who are still in touch—got together on a Zoom call for sort of a group counseling session. When triggered by an alarming event like this, people are not only reminded of their own unpleasant or downright hideous encounters, but also, it becomes the catalyst for remembering and analyzing our experiences from the past. Even in situations where many people shared the same environment, the experiences and memories of those moments are uniquely personal. In many cases, the negative or challenging experiences that some students endured went completely unnoticed by others. Whether they were kids commuting to our school from the city or Jewish kids going to Episcopalian school, or women in the first co-ed class in a previously all-male school, the difficulties were there but for the most part, unseen by many. If they were seen, most didn't want to talk about them, so how would others know? From a leadership perspective, as Tracy and Harland noted, avoiding the conversation is the antithesis of good leadership. You're running away from the reality of the workplace, not to mention the opportunity to educate, engage and inspire people. Sometimes, not knowing is easier than knowing because the depth of our dialog on delicate issues may be undeveloped and our bonds not yet strong enough to support the critical moments when empathy and understanding are needed.

That was the experience with my classmates during and after our Zoom call, which took place more than thirty years after we graduated. Stories of racism, intolerance, and bigotry were shared. They wanted to scream knowing the rest of us would finally hear their voices. I was frustrated that the treatment of some classmates by teachers and students alike (when we were fifteen years old) was unfair, and I remain frustrated today that I am unable to undo any of those situations. We can't change the past, but we can most definitely learn from it to make a positive impact in the future.

These same feelings come up within the workplace. When I first joined Hasbro, I wasn't from the toy industry, and I had the sense that some of my colleagues looked down on me as a result. Whether real or perceived, my feelings resulted in initial interactions that were sometimes awkward. It caused me to be guarded and less likely to speak up in certain situations. I see this as an example of unconscious bias. People may assume that because my background is not from the same industry, they directly or indirectly send signals that it will be difficult for me to be successful in the company. If people believe and convey to others that they won't be successful, they probably will not. When someone receives signals that they don't belong, how can they ever feel a sense of belonging? I saw this type of exchange a lot in the early stages of my career. As the organization became more purposely diverse in all aspects of its operation, being different became a superpower rather

Chapter 7

than a hindrance, and the organization recognized this as a key to its growth.

The world within an organization—which is sometimes a community and sometimes a universe, depending on your workplace— encompasses both colleagues and customers. There may be a thin line between the two, as Donna pointed out. We must be acutely aware of who we are as a company and who our consumers are. We must acknowledge it, speak it, see them, and see ourselves. This is the brand of belonging. When experienced, everyone buys in. Employees buy in with their time, their energy, and their engagement. Customers buy in with their money, their allegiance, and their reviews, shaping and upholding a brand's reputation for carrying these values through. Both buy in with their loyalty. With all this synergy, how can you lose?

Consider this win: With the goal of cementing the bond with a primary consumer base, in March 2021, Hennessy announced the selection of twenty esteemed inaugural members inducted into the "Never Stop Never Settle Society", a US$1 million program designed to champion the next generation of Black entrepreneurs in the United States. The initiative was introduced to support a more equitable landscape for inclusive business growth and development. The "Never Stop Never Settle Society" was built on Hennessy's long-standing commitment to Black communities, a legacy that dates back to the 1800s through a spectrum of investments and the sponsorship of civic organizations to enhance community development. The program was co-created with partner Marcus Graham Project, a nonprofit organization that shares Hennessy's mission to support diverse talent and leadership through funding and resources to drive meaningful growth. The twenty members were chosen for their commitment to reshaping the world through social impact, increasing representation in otherwise underrepresented spaces for Black-owned businesses, and job creation within their communities. Each member was provided US$50,000, access to professional development sessions with Moët Hennessy executives, and a membership to The Gathering Spot Connect, a Black-owned digital community offering culturally relevant content, networking, and business development resources. Members gained access to a state-of-the-art physical office at the Moët Hennessy headquarters in New York City. How amazing and inspirational!

Brands must become one with their audience. This doesn't mean you have to look just like them or share their lived experiences. There should be resonance and a recognition—even if a fraction of a high-profile allegiance like "Never Stop Never Settle Society".

Bonding with the Board

As an ally and contributor to women's initiatives and inclusive leadership through my association with Simmons University Institute for Inclusive Leadership Strategic Advisory Board, I sometimes experience imposter syndrome. However, if you consider their mission of "sharing the deep desire to foster equity, inclusion, and gender parity in organizational leadership in our lifetime as a 'global dream team of change-makers'", then there is no disconnection between them and me! Seriously, though, let's get real about not feeling perfectly qualified *all the time*. It's okay.

Several years ago, I participated in a conference produced by Odyssey Media, which catered to developing the careers of women of color. The host had assembled numerous participants to this inspirational, engaging conference for a day of learning and mentoring. To experience the energy in that room…WOW! Because of my role at Moët Hennessy, I was invited to participate and speak. It was intimidating, at first, because these women were so accomplished and confident. I didn't feel like I fit in. I was the only White man. Powerhouse Fox News journalist Arthel Neville interviewed me at the event, and the first question she asked caught me off guard: Which brand of LVMH do you most associate with? LVMH has over seventy-five brands. I said, "I enjoy most the celebration element, the gathering together. A brand I wear, Berluti, has a very rich history and is founded by a woman." It wasn't rehearsed. It reminded me of how important my personal connection was to some of the brands of LVMH, where I was pursuing my craft and career.

I was happy about my participation and I received positive feedback from the participants. I didn't go there with talking points or key takeaways, I just spoke openly and honestly about my life and leadership experience, which the attendees found relatable. When you do only this, your bonds will multiply.

Being surrounded by accomplished women can be a daunting experience, but it's incredibly enlightening to put yourself into situations where you are the minority. I'm already introverted in a group of strangers, let alone a gathering of brilliant women.

On the advisory board I serve, which is led by Susan Brady, CEO of Simmons University Institute for Inclusive Leadership, there are approximately twenty people. "Even as" the global head of DEI of an iconic company like LVMH bringing an array of experience and interests (or as a well-documented, well-quoted CEO or megastar pop singer), the humanness supersedes, the traits like vulnerability and insecurity kick in.

Upon our first meeting in person, Susan—in her conversational, amiable and inclusive approach—asked members of the board to share their experiences with imposter syndrome. I recounted a time when I was first asked to do this DEI role at Moët Hennessy, I had the feeling I would be found out! People would look to me to be an expert in a sensitive area that is ever evolving, sometimes uncomfortable and sometimes controversial, depending upon each individual's perceptions and life experiences. Over time, I have come to realize that the role is not about providing answers, but providing a path so others can arrive at their own answers.

This feeling is something constantly changing, related to someone's feelings and upbringing, and it includes psychology and corporate practice. Emotional intelligence (also known as emotional quotient or EQ) varies from one person to another. Some are born with more EQ than others, but those with a deficit can implement tools to manage their emotions in positive ways to demonstrate empathy, defuse conflict situations and relieve stress. The positive effects of team members with high EQ are cumulative.

Chapter 7

Let's be honest. Every time we say a word like "woke" or another that we know carries conflicting weight, it can challenge people. We have to listen more to the less vocal people who want to be included in the conversation and focus less on the ones who are screaming and demanding all of the airtime. Nobody wants to be marginalized. Everyone deserves to be part of the discussion. Leaving people out is a recipe for setting society back, not forward.

During a company training session I attended in Europe, one of the participants made a comment in reference to the statue of Robert E. Lee, one of the most celebrated and controversial generals of the American Civil War and leader of the Southern army. One program facilitator, who was European, responded to the comment by drawing from his own cultural references. He said to the group (which included many Americans), "You can't change history by taking statues down." This was a reference to the movement to remove statues celebrating the American Confederacy, a symbol to many of racism and separation. As leaders or as individuals representing a company, we have a responsibility to speak in a way that encourages and facilitates the creation of bonds. Whether someone believes it has context or significance, it's not part of the corporate dialogue to voice a personal, political view when acting on behalf of the company. I later discussed the comment with this individual by sharing, "When you made that comment, you alienated people in the room." He understood that what he said could be offensive to some of the participants. He learned from it, and I expect his delivery—while still charming and authentic as he is—will be more inclusive and apolitical in the future.

This type of situation is a reality of people's varied perspectives. Statues are symbols of honor, truth, history. I went to school in Virginia, and I didn't understand this until then because I grew up in the north of the United States in Pennsylvania, and remembrance of the Civil War, which had been fought 160 years earlier, was not a topic of conversation in day-to-day life. You have to meet people where they are, or you simply can't open dialogue.

Allyship: Let's Go There

After a very studious session on allyship that was conducted with our senior human resources team, I felt unsettled. Not because of the topic, but because it was missing the practical things an ally can do to actively support others. We're past the point of getting people to believe; now it's about action. I'm a man. How can I be a better ally to women? What am I actually doing and how am I engaging those I intend to support? How do I create an environment where everyone can succeed? Do I ask my colleagues how I can support them versus doing things that I believe create a feeling of inclusion? There may be some specific things I am doing or not doing to create that open safe space, or maybe I should exercise, "don't just stand there, do nothing!" Bottom line for me is, don't assume to know what is best for others when it comes to inclusion. Ask others. Invite them in so they can help me support them.

Tracy Spears, our "Shifting Out Loud" expert, said, "I'm weirdly open to anyone saying anything, trying it on and seeing if I can learn from it. I have a wide filter from the beginning. I'm listening for how I can connect to that person. I will be reading *HBR* and *People* at the same time. On the topic of CEOs, they say they don't want to make a mistake; they're afraid to say the wrong thing and don't even want to send emails anymore. Well, you're going to make mistakes and it humanizes you and endears people to you provided you circle back and talk about the mistake. That's a powerful piece to consider in the messaging you're crafting."

I consider how Tracy's advice can play out in different cultures. It's hard enough for a senior person in the West in an American company to get up and say, "Hey, I made a mistake and here's what I'm going to say, and it may not be alright." That would not happen in most Asian cultures. You'd completely lose face, and the assumption is that if you have the role and stand up that you always *know*. We talk about how Asian leaders can be effective in a French company. How a French person was raised to facilitate decision making may be the complete opposite, whereby the argument is an important part of the process of reaching a conclusion. I'm generalizing, of course, but I have witnessed it play out many times. Compare a system where a teacher tells students what is right and what is wrong and they write it down as fact to an interactive system where learning occurs through vigorous debate. Those two systems of deep programming are often difficult to reconcile within the workplace, reinforcing the need to ask the simple question of colleagues and team members, "How can I help you be successful?"

Several years ago, at Moët Hennessy, the leadership team launched a cultural change initiative. One of the components of the kick-off session, attended by every employee around the world over a series of months, was something called "no taboo". The employees could raise any question and a process was put in place to guarantee anonymity. Further to the questioning, employees were able to designate a representative who had the responsibility of holding up a red or green card, designating whether or not they believed the question had been sufficiently answered. There did not need to be agreement with the answer, just acceptance that it had been answered. It was a complete revolution for both management and employees alike. It was a very innovative means of showing the employees that the management was working to build a more open and inclusive culture, and it created more than a few anxious moments for everyone involved. I attended a session in Hong Kong the first a month after I joined the company and on that occasion, there were more than fifty questions submitted. Managers were very concerned that they would say the wrong thing, answer a question incorrectly or maybe worse, be challenged or publicly confronted on their answer. And you know what? Questions were answered hesitantly at first, sometimes mistakes were made, and from time to time, the leadership team was challenged on the responses. I had the good fortune of participating in numerous sessions across Asia Pacific. I witnessed firsthand how these remarkable moments of vulnerability resulted in deeper connections between managers and employees, opened up new lines of communication and created new ways of working together. Ultimately, these Q&A sessions became a mainstay in all employee forums.

Chapter 8
WE, THE DREAM TEAM

"Individually, we are one drop. Together, we are an ocean."

—*Ryunosuke Satoro, "father of the Japanese short story"*

IN MY FIRST week at Disney, we had diversity and inclusion training. I learned the basic concepts and what to watch out for. I was completely bought in. Let's just say I became an evangelist overnight. It was also a time in life when I was able to hear often limiting beliefs and skewed instructions, good intentions, even bad outcomes sometimes. In recent leadership positions, I've tried to evolve these early learnings. For example, ERGs are centered on specific underrepresented demographics. I believe it was the right approach then at Disney and Hasbro, but it has outlived its effectiveness. Back then, we could have an LGBTQ group of employees that were not making that much fundamental progress because it was effectively an echo chamber of the LGBT population talking to others in their community. It could become "woe is us" sessions. Don't get me wrong, it felt great to be in fellowship with people with whom I felt a connection on a very human level. These connections felt exclusive in terms of that community, but sometimes non-inclusive to allies. Again, here is where I grew as a lifetime learner. You don't evolve if you don't reflect, compare, and share! With this in mind, I now work together with employees and management teams to start with the ends of inclusion, innovation, and a stronger appreciation for customers and partners in mind. What does that mean in terms of actions? It necessitates everyone being part of the process. When this cultural change journey started, similar to what I have experienced in other organizations, about one-third of the people are all in. They are excited by the prospect of change, new ways of doing things, potential success, and learning. There are another one-third of employees who are willing to engage, yet they are going to wait to see if the movement is really going to change things or if it is another program without a chance to survive and be sustained. I would argue this is the target audience for change management and inclusion. Make this middle third feel invested, included, and heard and the game is won. Now about the final one-third. For them, the downsides of change are scary, unwanted, and can be viewed as unnecessary. Don't neglect these team members. Give them every chance to be included and heard. You may bring some to the middle or even, as I have seen, to the forefront as advocates for change and inclusion. Eventually, if the culture is really moving, these team members will vote by moving to the middle as advocates or leaving the organization. ERGs of underrepresented team members and their sponsors and allies have their place. In my view, however, they should not be the gateway to how fundamental change occurs. Everyone needs to be on the journey. No silos and no lonely souls.

A piece of advice someone gave me at Disney stands out. His perspective was, if you seek out alternate and diverse views and build a rapport with these people, you will go further faster. I was in my thirties, thirsty for the next thing, and I left a lot of relationship rubble behind me. I also missed out on a lot of strong support along the way. I was focused on whatever the "next thing" was, and I wasn't building long-term, mutually healthy relationships with colleagues. The next best thing is a bit of a drug—another promotion, a new job, increased responsibility…and *pause*! What am I doing here? Why am I doing this? I can remember the minutes of that conversation. This advice was so effective. Now, I practice relationship building, but initially I wasn't focused on that as a key skill.

I have also learned that nothing is more powerful than asking someone else for help and support. Making someone else feel included in your life, development, and growth is a powerful way to create bonds. It builds rapport, it allows that person to feel included and influential in your success. For the receiver, being asked to be a mentor, coach, or advisor is a gesture of respect, admiration, and recognition. Ask more, include more. Everyone wins.

At this point in my career, my life is driven by relationships and how my collective experience can be developed, enhanced, and passed on. It's no longer about politicking on the next step in my career. It's about how I'm going to make a difference in the company, in my community, and with people I care about.

Chapter 8

Do I attribute this mature stance to one's age? Personal growth? Independence? Depending upon the situation, it can be all of the above. In my case, I believe it is maturity through collective experiences, both successes and failures. It also comes with privilege. The perspective of a multicultural, multi-location, multi-generation company, with responsibility for diversity and inclusion, made me humbler. We should manage our expectations, given age and where our life is in general.

Circles, a Sodexo company, partners with organizations to cultivate an environment characterized by balance, engagement, and growth. In its Q1 2024 trends report covering "Workplace Insights and Trends in Work-Life Balance, Employee Well-being and Social Connection", one of the seven strategies to attract and retain talent in 2024 and beyond is: *Meet the needs of shifting generations in the workplace.* Let's understand the full scope of this. Circles explains, "While Baby Boomers dominated the workforce for decades, Generation Z has now surpassed them in number, and they're a very different generation from those before them. It's important to consider the generational makeup of your organization and to address generational differences when determining benefits."

Coming from the HR side, I know considering these generational differences can be tough. But this is a major element of diversity and inclusion. Again, it starts with mindset. We presently have the benefit and privilege of learning from all ages and vantage points. Why limit yourself by not drawing from the richness of human experience? If you see the range you can tap into like a globe, it spans oceans, mountainous terrain, countries, cultures, and colors. There is a constant flow and exchange for this varied knowledge in the workplace.

Circles advises, "Flexibility and listening will be the two cornerstones of effective lifestyle benefit planning for 2024, and beyond. Employees' needs shift as the environment shifts. It's important to stay attuned to what matters to your employees and to seek input from them to determine which benefits best meet these shifting needs. In this environment employers need to continually search for ways to help them stand out as an employer of choice to help them attract and retain top-notch employees. The right combination of lifestyle benefits can help."

When I reflect on those I've learned lessons from, the pool of influences ranges from the youngest, most zealous personalities to the many wise colleagues rooted in my parents' generation. Both of my parents lived in a collective dream team with everyone they touched. From a personality perspective, my father used to call himself a "goddamned jewel". He was self-deprecating, but he had a big personality and an oversized positive impact on others. Only at his funeral did I learn that he had mentored so many people. He preferred to spend his time with people who offered him perspective. He valued them, and those he mentored valued him. I now have a better understanding of where my passion for the same originated.

My mom spent a lifetime actively engaged in the community and as a board member for charitable organizations including The Emergency Aid of Pennsylvania, Inglis House, Philadelphia Hospitality, The Franklin Institute, the Cosmopolitan Club, and as a local and National Board Member of the American

Cancer Society where she played a leading role championing the restriction of smoking in public places.

I reflect on the magnitude of my parents' contributions to their communities and personal networks, to their version of the dream team, and it helps me stay focused on mine.

Shawn adds, "Throughout the time we've been together, Greg has volunteered as a mentor for countless students and junior colleagues. Even with some of the mentees from years ago, Greg is still in touch. He's frequently on calls with former mentees, and he'll even make it a point of seeing them in the city he visits. He genuinely cares about how people are developing, and he wants to know that they're thriving. It's so real, and I look to Greg for that. I've never seen mentorship in anyone else at that level. For Greg, it's a pleasure to help people grow and think about things differently—including himself."

When Bonding Is a Game

More than thirty ago, the first "Gay Days" were held at Walt Disney World in Orlando, Florida. In the early years of this event, which was not sponsored by Disney, the company would place letters in the guest rooms of every hotel, as well as signage at the front of the park alerting guests that it was a special event for the gay community. Moreover, the message stated that if anyone was uncomfortable with that, Disney would give them a pass to another park or a refund. I remember dealing with a family from Wisconsin in which the mother was overwhelmed and crying. She didn't have the exposure to understand how to explain the event to her children, and this is not what she expected for a day out at "the most magical place on earth". In talking with her, I could understand her fear for her children and her anger with having to deal with something unfamiliar. While I did not agree with her—nor did I expect from the expressions on her family's faces did they—I felt it was a lesson in humility, understanding, and forgiveness. I recall this moment often while working in the DEI space. Not everyone feels like a world of diversity, inclusion, and belonging is relevant or understandable to them. All the more reason to bring those individuals into your conversations early and often.

Gay Games, a nine-day sports and culture event held every four years at different locations around the world, is an interesting model of a dream team for a leader because it aims to create a sense of belonging in an organization where everyone is a volunteer. You must deeply engage people to join and gracefully say goodbye to them when they leave. I became involved to see more sport lovers turn into advocates and more fair, likeminded people to support an all-inclusive world through sports and entertainment.

Shawn and I attended Gay Games in Paris in the summer of 2018, as he was competing as a swimmer with several of his swim team friends. The spirit was incredible. You walk into a stadium on the pitch like a real Olympian and it's already mind-blowing. People are cheering. The sense of belonging and spirit sold it for me. I immediately volunteered to be part of the team to host Gay Games in Hong Kong in 2022!

During the event, I met two guys and a woman who had traveled from China to participate. Fortunately, one of the guys spoke English very well. With my typical curiosity, I asked, "Why did you come to Gay Games?" The three came from a city called Baotou near inner Mongolia. I've been there and it is a rather grim, grey place. It is where most of the rare earth metals in smartphones are mined, so pollution is high. He explained that by attending Gay Games they could attend an inclusive sports and arts and culture event and not have tell his family it was a gay event. Being out to his parents was not an option any of the three saw as possible. He shared that they never thought they would ever be in an environment that was so welcoming, inclusive, and happy. The sense of hope from that event became so powerful in their lives. I thought, if one person or ten people or more could have that feeling of belonging, then I was all in and my contribution would be worth it. I share the Gay Games experience from Paris because it was such a strong lesson to me about inclusion and belonging.

On a quest to bring Gay Games to Hong Kong, I worked with a team of dedicated individuals over the time I was associated with the project. The founder, Dennis Philipse, co-chairs Lisa Lam and Alan Lang, among many others. The organizing team had one challenge after another: resistance from certain public officials, protests, and COVID-19, to name a few. Christian booths were thrown up around the proposed locations to try to persuade the government to stop the event, but the Games amassed significant corporate and community support, which won in the end. When Lisa started as a Gay Games volunteer, she was responsible for legal matters and government relations. When the role of co-chair became available, Lisa was asked to consider it. She was hesitant because she wasn't sure she had the same level of commitment as others, specifically as it related to leading a major global sporting event. Her view was that the lasting positive impact on the LGBT community in Hong Kong was the primary goal, and the sporting events themselves were a means to an end. Historically, sports had often been off limits to gay people so when you create that safe space in a place that doesn't normally seem like it is home for LGBTQ people, then it's very enabling. It reinforces that we can all be part of the same world.

Breakthroughs can make inclusion surge. The Gay Games movement is more about participation and personal best than it is about winning a medal, even though some people train for years and take the competition extremely seriously. Participants and volunteers feel respected and included within a safe space. People will always find a reason to exclude, but inclusion is a lot more fun.

Keys to Connection

Lisa Lam on Creating Dream Teams

Lisa Lam is a legal and regulatory compliance practitioner with over twenty years of experience in the digital finance sector. As Gay Games co-chair, Lisa broke through barriers to change the paradigm and culture that she came out of. That's so powerful. The first big event of "coming out" for Hong Kong Gay Games was World Pride in Sydney, Australia. Lisa was all over the news in Asia defending the Games. Her understated way masks a deep passion and vision. She sees well beyond this as a sporting event, linking connection to purpose.

When I first spoke to Lisa for this book, Gay Games had ten months to go before opening day! Venues had been confirmed, which was a massive undertaking in and of itself. I consider Lisa's keys to connection a positive historical record, among a modern-day view on belonging and bonds.

Reach outside your comfort zone for allies.

In this work, the one thing that impressed me is the work of building allyship and spreading the word beyond the queer community. It's about increasing acceptance level and reaching outside. In the last year, we drew more and more people outside of Games and joining as volunteers. I got this mother who joined who has a three-year-old boy who referred to the news of gay youth committing suicide after all this pressure by family and friends. She joined in thinking about her young son—that if he were gay. If all mothers could be like her, we could just fold up Gay Games and go home. We don't need it. We're seeing people believing in the cause.

Find relevance in other communities and causes to feel a greater sense of belonging.

More people from Asia joined. They heard the message. We made a deliberate effort and gave ourselves metrics in how we invest resources. In the two years leading up to the Games, we asked ourselves, "What are we doing to lift that purpose?" We had targeted KPIs. We wanted to make sure we had Asians, more women, as well as transgender community representation. We wanted to make sure we were mindful and deliberate toward volunteers or the way we conducted the Games. In order to do that, we had local outreach activities. We had Games at the Hong Kong University of Science and Technology. That was to target college mainstream. Over 400 participated in a weekend event in squash, volleyball, and table tennis. Students from six universities sent their teams. It was about sending the message and having a large educational institution endorse it.

Stay motivated by learning everything you can about your cause, constituents, opponents—even historical context.

I was born and raised in Hong Kong. I joined Gay Games in 2018, had semi-retired in 2017 at age fifty. I was growing up in the '70s and '80s in

Hong Kong when the word *lesbian* was not in the vocabulary. My parents are very loving, I had a very good family. I decided enough corporate. I wanted to reexamine how I live. I wanted to find a cause to stand for and volunteer for. A friend said, the Gay Games were looking for a lawyer. I took quite a bit of work on the government relations side and spent time on local outreach. This was the first time in Hong Kong, first time in Asia.

Historically, if you look at Chinese culture, being queer is not something you really talk about. Even some of our famous classics talk about gay love. What I do find is that in the last 150 years, I do see remnants of being a colony and Christianity. Being a colony cuts off the roots. That's why you find an interesting mix in how people like my parents, who are not religious, still had certain values. In the past, at a societal level, it was very hard. There was no language. If you look at research, a Chinese university professor did a study on public attitudes in 2016—do you support legal protection for LGBT? Hong Kong has an equal opportunities ordinance, which set up various grounds of discrimination, and sexual orientation was not one of them. Legally, you could discriminate against queer people. In 2016, 35 percent of respondents said, "Yes, we support protections for LGBTQ+ people." That's a big chunk of society that didn't support inclusive protections. In 2019, researchers asked the same question and 60 percent said "yes". If you look at the age cohort of 18-34, over 80 percent said "yes." That's very encouraging. Hong Kong is safe to begin with. You don't see rampant violent crime. You can see the younger generation much more expressive. COVID-19 helped—meaning, wearing masks and feeling bolder, displaying affection.

All of these are encouraging signs, but there's still that 40 percent saying "no". Maybe 10 percent never will. But if they see more positive images, maybe they will. For nine days, you'll have people from all around the world descending on Hong Kong. We have thirty locations. This is bound to change the industry. You get in a taxi and people wearing Gay Games tag. I hope people see it's just fun. There is nothing unusual or weird. That kind of visibility and representation. We had an event on a Wednesday in the summer at Water World Park, amusement park, which has been around for forty years. It was a whole day. We invited sponsors, volunteers, and community partners to play on the water slides. Everyone together with their families. We also invited the equal opportunities chairperson to give a speech. We went to the management of the park and asked them to arrange for gender-neutral facilities, including changing rooms.

One volunteer, an ally, went in with his sister and brother-in-law and one-and-a-half-year-old baby. The security guard assumed he and his brother-in-law were a couple and the baby was their child, and the woman was in a separate group.

> Impressive for Hong Kong! Can you say you don't know a gay person anymore? We try to dissect the biases with this competitive and fun event in a major international city.

Personal growth is exhilarating.

Personally, I learned a lot. I'm quite inspired. I don't even play sports. On an intellectual level, it's very interesting for me to learn all these things, but fundamentally it's meeting all these people from all walks of life and hearing their stories and working together because we believe in something. This is a multi-year relay. There was work from previous volunteers carrying over into other volunteer work. It's very empowering seeing it happening that we can carry so much so far. When you believe in something and work at it one day at a time, it keeps you motivated.

I always ask myself about the purpose and why I joined. That is very important to me. Success is not about those nine days—it's the journey, impact, and legacy. Ultimately, I need to deliver those nine days, but creating the energy with the people who believe in that cause, common goal and shared mission and delivering it. There are a lot of talented people in Hong Kong. We had to find those people to help us deliver it! I have total faith in them. We

> see universities, schools, and pubs giving them their settings. This energy feeds everyone.

> **Feeling like you belong opens the door for everything else in life.**
> I want everyone to feel okay and that I'm okay. It's a simple thing. To be able to feel that I'm okay. That would be my dream. It's modest. I'm always coming back to why I have these motivations. I'm open to ideas. Why do I have that in me internally? I was very lucky to have my parents, who have so much trust and gave me so much room to explore who I am. I always felt okay as myself even though I couldn't verbalize it. Inclusion matters; it's okay to be you. Mental health is so important—always look out for yours.

Shawn and I traveled back to Hong Kong to support our friends and participate in the experience. Around 3,000 athletes participated in Gay Games Hong Kong, the first in the organization's forty-year history to be held in Asia. It was everything we dreamed: inclusive, inspiring, emotional, difficult, and a lot of fun. The net impact beyond the extremely positive experiences of visitors and sorely needed financial and tourism boost was the encouragement and building of a strong community of LGBTQ people and their allies. This is the legacy of inclusion and belonging, which will only grow stronger.

Chapter 9
SAFE AND CELEBRATED

"The really wonderful thing that happened to me when I was in space was this feeling of belonging to the entire universe."

—*Mae Jemison, astronaut*

LEADERS TOUCH PEOPLE from a lot of different worlds. How will they carry on your legacy? Each person you come in contact with can be meaningful. The relationship with each is unique. I find that so enriching.

It's so important that people in an organization always know where their home base is. How do we help people find that, especially when they're new in an organization? How do I fit in and still be myself? You can be at any career level, any location, asking yourself these same questions…and know someone else is contemplating the same. There is some sense of safety in this thought.

Chapter 9

I have learned a lot from my friend, Emery Fung, in Hong Kong, who is transgender. Listening to his transformational stories about transitioning, the gravity of his circumstances hit me in the gut with a force—of empathy. First, no one walks into a clinic after a binger overnight and says, "I want a new body!" It's not a marriage in Vegas. Understand the magnitude of impact on someone's body, family, and life. Emery explained, "I spent months deliberating when I was going to change my LinkedIn profile." I should note that his profession was recruiting, and LinkedIn is a key part of generating your income and livelihood. It's your persona. He had to change from who "she" was to who he is and somehow explain that. Most outside his family, including close friends and his partner, didn't know he was going through this process or even struggling with being transgender. Then the first time he had to shop and pick out a men's razor to shave new, textured hair with—this is a basic function, but remember, he's been shopping in the women's aisle for razors. The woman working in the store came over and graciously offered her assistance. Those moments these strangers spent together in a mundane store aisle were vulnerable and victorious. He has surrounded himself with positivity and it is his safe space. He has created a resource for DEI professionals in Asia at www.emeryfung.com. He is building inclusive spaces from his own experience. If Emery can do it, we all can.

Describing the neuroscience of human connections in 2013, scientist Matthew Lieberman said, "At businesses worldwide, pay for performance is just about the only incentive used to motivate employees. However, praise and an environment free from social threats are also powerful motivators. Because social pain and pleasure haven't been a part of our theory of 'who we are' we tend not to use these social motivators as much as we could."

As I reflect on this more than a decade later, I'm so glad to see more businesses visibly offer a premium on the psychological safety that brings forth the absolute pleasure of one's company and steps closer to the bonds that are unbreakable. The bonds start with individuals. You and me. Every interaction that we have with another human unlocks the door to wisdom and emotional resonance. We never have to go to a locksmith for duplicates of the keys to inclusion and connection because our curiosity and empathy will always let us in. As we step in, we gain a greater sense of who we are and let others in to share in this amazing experience of life. We thrive together.

References

Interviews

Harland Chun. Zoom. January 19, 2023.

Shawn Hiltz. Zoom. August 9, 2023.

Lisa Lam. Zoom. January 26, 2023.

Patricia Morley. Zoom. August 9, 2023.

Tracy Spears. Zoom. January 11, 2023.

Donna Wilson. Zoom. January 11, 2023.

Publications

Alancheril, Jane. "Thinking Like a CFO." *Gartner*. PowerPoint Presentation.

Allen, Summer. "How Biology Prepares Us for Love and Connection." *Greater Good Magazine*. February 24, 2022.

https://greatergood.berkeley.edu/article/item/ how_biology_prepares_us_for_love_and_connection.

Bailinson, Peter, William Decherd, Diana Ellsworth, and Maital Guttman. "LGBTQ+ Voices: Learning from Lived Experiences." *McKinsey & Company.* June 25, 2020.

https://www.mckinsey.com/capabilities/people-and-organizational-performance/our-insights/ lgbtq-plus-voices-learning-from-lived-experiences.

Bator, David. "The Power of Belonging—Creating an Inclusive and Productive Workforce." *Achievers Workforce Institute.* PowerPoint Presentation.

Born This Way Foundation. "Our Impact."

https://bornthisway.foundation/ourimpact/.

Bossart, Celine. "Lady Gaga on Her Latest Dom Pérignon Collaboration." *Cool Hunting.* March 22, 2023.

https://coolhunting.com/culture/ interview-lady-gaga-dom-perignon/.

Bourke, Juliet, and Bernadette Dillon. "The Diversity and Inclusion Revolution." *Deloitte Review.* Issue 22, January 2018.

https://www2.deloitte.com/content/dam/insights/us/ articles/4209_Diversity-and-inclusion-revolution/DI_ Diversity-and-inclusion-revolution.pdf.

Chen, Te-Ping. "The Rise and Fall of the Chief Diversity Officer." *The Wall Street Journal.* July 21, 2023.

https://www.wsj.com/articles/chief-diversity-officer-cdo-business-corporations-e110a82f?mod=hp_lead_pos9.

Circles. "Q1 2024 Trends: Workplace Insights and Trends in Work-Life Balance, Employee Well-being and Social Connection." *Circles US.* PDF Download, Subscriber-Based.

Cook, Gareth. "Why We Are Wired to Connect." *Scientific American.* October 22, 2013.

https://www.scientificamerican.com/article/why-we-are-wired-to-connect/.

Davis, Tchiki. "Develop Authenticity: 20 Ways to Be a More Authentic Person." *Psychology Today.* April 15, 2019.

https://www.psychologytoday.com/us/blog/click-here-happiness/201904/develop-authenticity-20-ways-be-more-authentic-person.

Dixon-Fyle, Sundiatu, Kevin Dolan, Dame Vivian Hunt, and Sara Prince. "Diversity Wins: How Inclusion Matters." *McKinsey & Company.* May 19, 2020.

https://www.mckinsey.com/featured-insights/diversity-and-inclusion/diversity-wins-how-inclusion-matters.

Fagaly, Matt. "The 5 Types of Leadership Styles That Can Define Your Organization's Culture. *BK Connection.* March 13, 2018.

https://ideas.bkconnection.com/the-5-types-of-leadership-styles-that-can-define-your-organizations-culture.

Harper, Rose. "How Does Empathy Vary Across Different Cultures?" *Morgan Latif Insight.* November 3, 2023.

https://morganlatif.com/insight/how-does-empathy-vary-across-different-cultures/.

Hennessy. "Hennessy Unveils 2021 Inaugural Members of 'Never Stop Never Settle Society,' An Initiative for Black Entrepreneurs." *Hennessy/PR Wire.* August 24, 2021.

https://www.prnewswire.com/news-releases/hennessy-unveils-2021-inaugural-members-of-never-stop-never-settle-society-an-initiative-for-black-entrepreneurs-301361666.html.

Horowitz, Juliana Menasce, and Kim Parker. "How Americans View Their Jobs." Pew Research Center. March 30, 2023.

https://www.pewresearch.org/social-trends/2023/03/30/how-americans-view-their-jobs/.

Ignition Coaching. "Companies With Excellent Employee Retention Strategies." *Ignition Coaching Blog.*

https://www.ignition-coaching.com/blog/companies-with-excellent-employee-retention-strategies.

Ipsos. "Americans Divided on Whether 'Woke' is a Compliment or Insult." *Ipsos.* March 8, 2023.

https://www.ipsos.com/en-us/americans-divided-whether-woke-compliment-or-insult.

Lahey, Jesse. "3 Risks of Authentic Leadership." *Engaging Leader.*

https://engagingleader.com/the-power-of-authenticity/.

Leung, Kanis. "Supporters celebrate opening of Gay Games in Hong Kong, first in Asia, despite lawmakers' opposition." *AP News.* November 4, 2023.

https://apnews.com/article/hong-kong-gay-games-lgbtq-opposition-dfcabada2fc9eb95f61ee5788e0c2c61.

Long, Britta. "Build Connection in the Workplace." *Insight Global.* March 23, 2023.

https://insightglobal.com/blog/build-connection-in-workplace/.

McKinsey & Company. "Diversity and Inclusion." *Featured Insights.*

https://www.mckinsey.com/featured-insights/diversity-and-inclusion.

Murthy, Vivek. "Work and the Loneliness Epidemic." *Harvard Business Review.* September 26, 2017.

https://hbr.org/2017/09/work-and-the-loneliness-epidemic?utm_medium=paidsearch&utm_source=google&utm_campaign=domcontent&utm_term=Non-Brand&tpcc=paidsearch.google.dsacontent&gad_source=1&gclid=Cj0KCQiAnrOtBhDIARIsAFsSe525gNAB3UABb26ru4-frADopOxuNQSxDaiXsGgoy7Rd3T7cUsi6kgcaAjojEALw_wcB.

Nicolaou, Elena, and Courtney E. Smith. "A #MeToo Timeline to Show How Far We've Come—and How Far We Need to Go." *Refinery 29.* October 5, 2019.

https://www.refinery29.com/en-us/2018/10/212801/me-too-movement-history-timeline-year-weinstein.

Rodriguez, Adrianna. "Americans are lonely and it's killing them. How the US can combat this new epidemic." *USA Today.* December 24, 2023.

https://www.usatoday.com/story/news/health/2023/12/24/loneliness-epidemic-u-s-surgeon-general-solution/71971896007/.

Shardlow, Estella. "Gen Proactive: A Guide to Galvanized Global Youth." *Stylus/Consumer Attitudes.* April 13, 2022. PDF.

Singler, Emily. "Embracing stories in the practice of veterinary medicine." *AAHA.org.* February 2, 2023.

https://www.aaha.org/publications/newstat/articles/2023-2/embracing-stories-in-the-practice-of-veterinary-medicine/.

Taylor, Astra. "Why Does Everyone Feel So Insecure All the Time?" *The New York Times.* August 18, 2023.

https://www.nytimes.com/2023/08/18/opinion/inequality-insecurity-economic-wealth.html?campaign_id=190.

Tyagi, Srishti. "The Science of Human Bonding." *The Cornell Daily Sun.* February 13, 2020.

https://cornellsun.com/2020/02/13/the-science-of-human-bonding/.

Yeung, Jessie, and Moeri Karasawi. "Japan was already grappling with isolation and loneliness. The pandemic made it worse." CNN. April 7, 2023.

https://edition.cnn.com/2023/04/06/asia/japan-hikikomori-study-covid-intl-hnk/index.html.

About the Author

Greg Morley is most recently Global Head of Diversity, Equity and Inclusion for Moët Hennessy, a division of LVMH. Greg brings a personal and professional passion to the development of talent and to helping others achieve more than they believe they can. Greg led the HR function for the company's operations across the Asia Pacific region. Prior to joining Moët Hennessy, he was Vice President, Human Resources Asia Pacific for Hasbro, Inc. and was Vice President, Human Resources for the Shanghai Disney Resort. He has been based in Hong Kong, Paris, and the US for The Walt Disney Company, starting his career in General Electric.

Greg played a leading role in the team that brought the 2024 Gay Games, a global-participant sports, culture, and diversity event, to Asia for the first time in its 40-year history, specifically to Hong Kong.

Printed in the USA
CPSIA information can be obtained
at www.ICGtesting.com
LVHW091331310824
789811LV00035B/629